Succeed in
Cambridge English
Preliminary

Preliminary English Test (PET)

10
Practice Tests

GlobalELT
ENGLISH LANGUAGE TEACHING BOOKS

Succeed in
Cambridge English
Preliminary
Preliminary English Test (PET)

The **Cambridge English Preliminary English Test** (PET) is the second level Cambridge ESOL exam. It is an intermediate level exam, at Level B1 of the Council of Europe's Common European Framework of Reference for Languages. It tests whether candidates are able to read simple texts and articles, write simple personal letters, make notes during a meeting or understand everyday dialogues or monologues.

PET is a very useful qualification as it is widely recognised in international business. It is also useful preparation for other Cambridge ESOL exams, such as FCE, CAE and CPE.

The certificate is recognised by employers in many countries. It is also recognised by some universities as an initial qualification in English.

Published by GLOBAL ELT LTD
www.globalelt.co.uk
email: orders@globalelt.co.uk

Copyright © **GLOBAL ELT LTD**, 2011

British Library Cataloguing-in-Publication Data
A catalogue record of this book is available from the British Library.
● Succeed in PET - 10 Practice Tests - Student's Book - ISBN: 978-1-904663-23-2
● Succeed in PET - 10 Practice Tests - Teacher's Book - ISBN: 978-1-904663-24-9

Every effort has been made to trace the copyright holders and we apologise in advance for any unintentional omission.
We will be happy to insert the appropriate acknowledgements in any subsequent editions.

The authors and publishers wish to acknowledge the following use of material:
Art Explosion Cliparts (in the speaking section: p. 6-16) and the photos in Tests: 1,5, 6,7 8 © Nova Development Corporation
The photos in Tests: 2, 3, 7, 9, 10 (in the speaking section: p. 6-16) © Ingram Publishing Image Library

CONTENTS

CONTENTS

Cambridge English
Preliminary
Preliminary English Test (PET)

Paper	Time	Content	Test Focus
Paper 1 Reading / Writing	1 hour 30 minutes	**Reading:** Five parts. Various reading skills are tested through a selection of texts ranging from very short notices to extended texts. **Writing:** Three parts. A variety of writing skills are tested.	Evaluation of candidates' understanding of written English at the levels of individual words, phrases, sentences, paragraphs and whole texts. Evaluation of candidates' written English skills, from rephrasing simple sentences to producing continuous text.
Paper 2 Listening	30 minutes	Four parts. Listening skills are tested through short and long conversations and speeches.	Evaluation of candidates' understanding of informal and general dialogues and monologues on common topics.
Paper 3 Speaking	10—12 minutes	**Four parts:** **Part 1:** candidates speak with the examiner **Part 2:** candidates speak to each other **Part 3:** extended individual speaking **Part 4:** candidates speak to each other	Evaluation of candidates' basic expression in English, including asking and responding to questions and discussing their lives and experiences.

Speaking Section

Paper 3

Practice Tests: 1-10

Speaking Test 1

Part 2

Starting a hobby

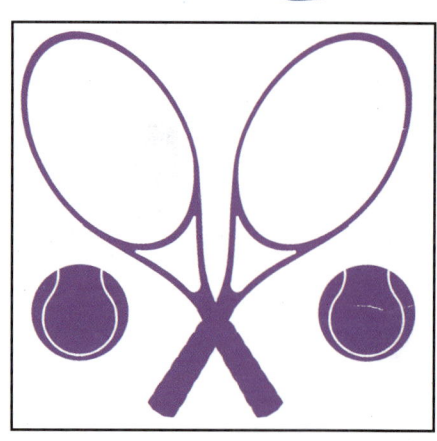

Photograph A
Candidate A

Part 3

Photograph B
Candidate B

Speaking Test 2

Part 2

Starting a youth club

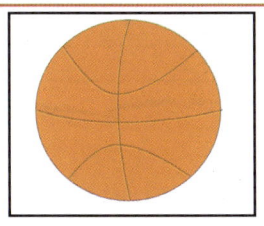

Photograph A
Candidate A

Part 3

Photograph B
Candidate B

Photograph C
Candidate C

Speaking Test 3

Part 2

Journey in a car

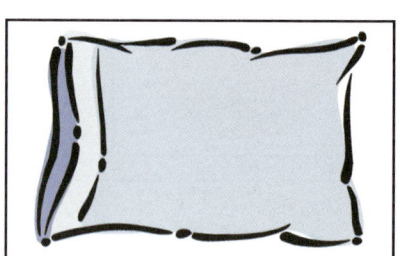

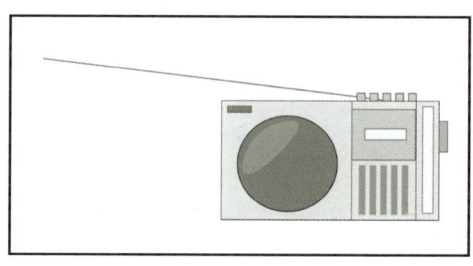

Part 3

Photograph A
Candidate A

Photograph B
Candidate B

Speaking Test 4

Part 2

School trip

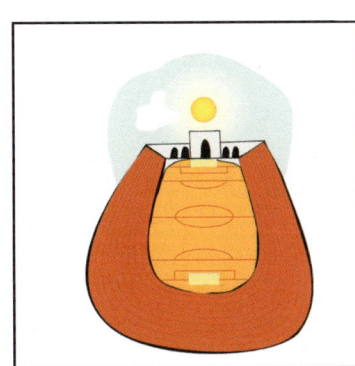

Part 3

Photograph A
Candidate A

Photograph B
Candidate B

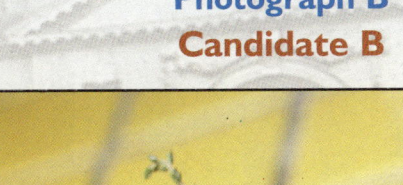

Speaking Test 5

Part 2

Choosing the best job

Part 3

Photograph A
Candidate A

Photograph B
Candidate B

Speaking Test 6

Part 2

Camping holiday

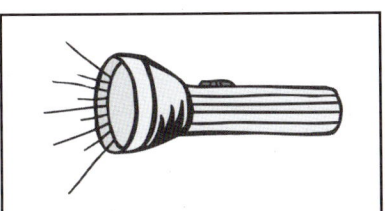
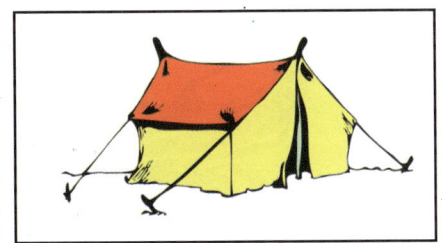
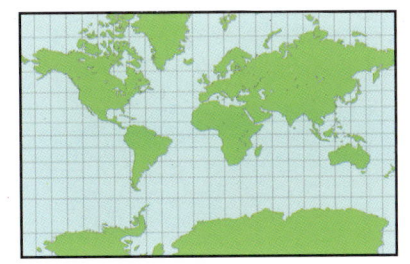
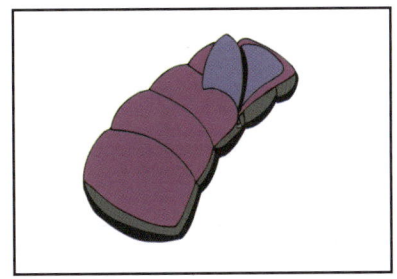

Part 3

Photograph A
Candidate A

Photograph B
Candidate B

Part 2 **Speaking Test 7**

Mother's Day present

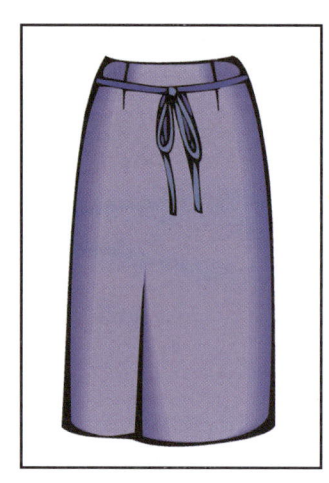
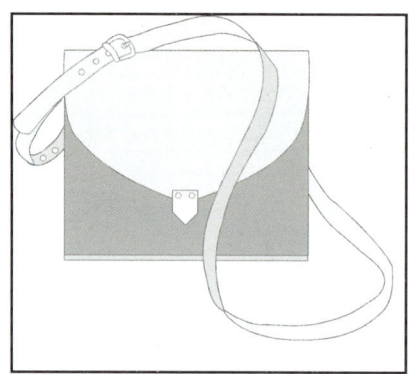
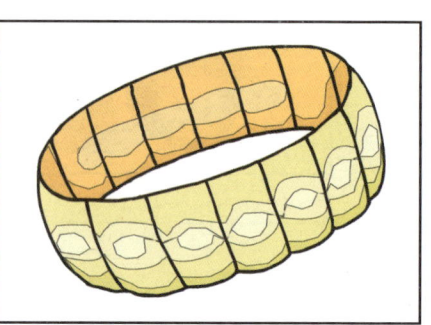

Part 3

Photograph A
Candidate A

Photograph B
Candidate B

Photograph C
Candidate C

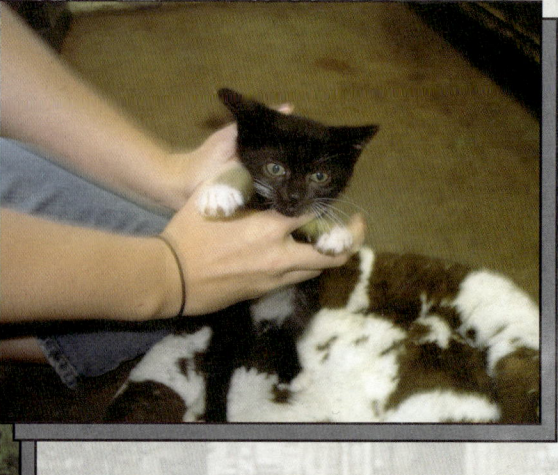

Part 2

Speaking Test 8

Visit from a friend

Photograph A
Candidate A

Part 3

Photograph B
Candidate B

Part 2   **Speaking Test 9**

Interesting class

LITERATURE

COMPUTERS

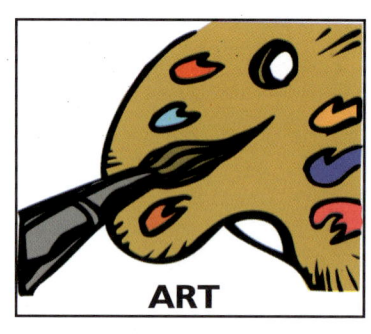

ART

MATHS

CHEMISTRY

MUSIC

Photograph A
Candidate A

Part 3

Photograph B
Candidate B

Part 2   ## Speaking Test 10

Your favourite pet

Photograph A
Candidate A

Part 3

Photograph B
Candidate B

The Speaking Test

The Speaking test is about 10 to 12 minutes long. Candidates take the test in pairs. There are two examiners, one who talks to you and one who listens to you. You receive marks from both examiners.

Part 1

The examiners tell you their names and one examiner asks you and the other candidate what your names are and how you spell them. Then this examiner asks you about yourself, your daily life, interests, activities etc.

Part 2

The examiner asks you and the other candidate to talk about a topic together and gives you a picture to help you get ideas.

Part 3

Now you and your partner each talk on your own. The examiner asks you to talk about a colour photograph which you are given. After you finish talking, the examiner asks the other candidate to talk about a different photograph.

Part 4

The examiner asks you and your partner to discuss the subject of the photographs you were given in Part 3. This may include giving your opinion or talking about personal experiences.

Part 1

General questions about yourself, interests, hobbies, etc.

- What's your name?
- Where do you live?
- What is your home like?
- Do you live in a house or a flat?
- Do you like the area you live in? Why (not)?
 - Can you spell the name of your street?

- Can you tell me about your family?
- Do you have a large or small family?
- Can you tell me something about your family?

- What did you do on Sunday?
- What did you do yesterday evening / last weekend?
- What are you going to do at the weekend?
- Do you have any hobbies?
- What do you enjoy doing in your free time?
- Where did you go on holiday last year?

- What do you like to watch on TV?
- Which do you prefer more, watching TV or going to the cinema?
- Do you enjoy playing or watching any sport?

- Do you work or are you a student in …?
- What are/were your favourite subjects at school?
- What subjects do you study?
- Have you got a job?
- What job do you do?

- Do you enjoy studying English? Why (not)?
- How long have you been learning English?
- Why is it important for you to learn English?
- How important is English for your future plans?
- What do you hope to be doing in five years' time?
- Is there anywhere in particular that you would like to visit?

Cambridge English
Preliminary

Preliminary English Test **PET**

PRACTICE

TESTS

The **Justification of the Answers** for the **Reading** and the **Listening Sections** can be found in the **Self-study Guide.**

Test 1

PAPER 1 READING & WRITING

PART 1   Questions 1-5

Look at the text in each question. What does it say? Mark the letter next to the correct explanation **A, B** or **C.**

Example:

0

> **NO BALL GAMES ALLOWED ON THE GRASS**

A. You may not sit on the grass.
B. Be careful not to damage the grass while playing ball games on it.
C. All ball games are forbidden on the grass.

Example answer: **0** | **C**

1

> **Do not lean out of the train window**

C

A. You must not open the window.
B. The windows do not open.
C. You must not put your head out of the window.

2

> Smoking is only allowed in the smoking areas.

B

A. You are not allowed to smoke anywhere in the building.
B. There are certain places where you can smoke.
C. You must smoke if you are in this area.

3

> **E-mail**
> **To:** Ben
> **From:** Mark
> The tennis match will be cancelled if it is raining and we'll go to the cinema instead.

C

A. They are not going to play tennis.
B. They will go to the cinema.
C. They may not play tennis.

4

> **Do not open the door until the red light has gone off and the green light comes on**

A

A. Wait for the green light before opening the door.
B. Turn off the red light when you open the door.
C. Do not open the door when the green light is on.

5

> **Message**
> **To:** Anne
> **From:** Julie
> *Anne, your doctor's appointment is at two o'clock on Monday instead of three o'clock on Tuesday*

B

Anne's appointment
A. will be a day later.
B. will no longer be on Tuesday.
C. will be an hour later.

PART 2 | **Questions 6-10**

These people (6-10) want to stay home and watch TV tonight. Below there are some TV programme reviews (A-H). Decide which programme (**letters A-H**) would be the most suitable for each person (**numbers 6-10**). Write the correct letter for each number.

6. Brian likes watersports very much. He would like to go sailing next summer with his friends. He works in a shop and doesn't have much money.

7. Sally is a very romantic person. She likes watching programmes about real people and their lives. She is particularly interested in programmes about people who have coped with problems in their life.

8. Dave is a geography teacher in a secondary school in Liverpool. He likes programmes about travel and the environment in general. He is also very interested in wildlife.

9. Jane is a very artistic person. She enjoys making things and painting in her free time. She enjoys visiting art galleries and museums.

10. Simon works in a bank and is very interested in finance and politics. He likes to read the newspaper everyday and to be aware of what is going on in the world.

6	C

7	H

8	A

9	F

10	B

TV PROGRAMMES

A. "The World Around Us"
A fascinating study of the ancient Egyptian pyramids and the area around the River Nile in Egypt. The scenery is beautiful and the filming of this documentary is a work of art as it is so thoughtfully done. As well as the obvious camels, there are also many interesting images of other desert animals and plant life.

B. "Speak Up"
Well-known personalities discuss the main stories of the day. What is going on in the government and who is attacking who in the political parties. Always a lively programme as events, both at home and abroad, are debated with great enthusiasm.

C. "Summer Holidays"
A practical and honest account of some of the summer holidays that are on offer this year. Tonight's programme features a weekend in Disneyland in Paris, cheap sailing holidays in the Mediterranean and a shopping and sightseeing trip to New York.

D. "Cooking for special occasions"
The fun cookery programme that offers lots of exciting ideas from children's birthday parties to that frightening dinner for the boss and his wife. Easy to follow step by step instructions and many useful tips on how to make your dinner party a little bit special.

E. "The weather programme"
All your weather forecasts in one programme. Featuring local, national and international weather news, this is a handy programme for anyone who is about to travel or go on holiday. So if you are off on a trip or have an outside event planned, don't miss this informative programme.

F. "The Creative Mind"
One of the most popular programmes on TV at the moment, *The Creative Mind* explores different artistic themes from exhibition reviews, information about major and smaller galleries and museums, and interviews with artists, writers, actors and musicians.

G. "Death in Paris"
A fast, violent film about the Mafia in Paris. Although there are some good actors in this film, the story isn't very exciting or interesting and it is often hard to understand what is going on. There are some beautiful Parisian scenes however and a few funny moments between the scenes of violence.

H. "Born to Run"
An interesting story of a young man with learning difficulties who overcame the problems in his life, through his great talent for athletics. This is a true story of how one person made the most of their life and also helped many other people with similar problems. The happy ending will appeal to all those romantics out there.

PAPER 1 – READING

Look at the statements below about holidays in and around the city of Norwich in England. Read the text below to decide if each statement is correct or incorrect. If it is correct, mark **A**. If it is incorrect, mark **B**.

11. There are only a lot of tourists in Norwich in the summer.

| 11 | B |

12. You don't have to pay a lot of money to stay in Norwich.

| 12 | A |

13. All your meals are included in the cost of a room at the Beeches Hotel.

| 13 | B |

14. It is cheaper to stay at the Beeches Hotel in the winter.

| 14 | A |

15. "The Cathedral" is the name of a theatre in Norwich.

| 15 | B |

16. Anyone can go to the "Fire from Heaven" show.

| 16 | A |

17. The Sainsbury Centre has art from all over the world.

| 17 | A |

18. If you don't eat meat, you shouldn't eat in the Sainsbury Centre canteen.

| 18 | B |

19. You can save a lot of money at the factory shoe shops.

| 19 | A |

20. The Broads are not really suitable for a family holiday.

| 20 | B |

"Holidays in Norwich"

Norwich is the capital of East Anglia, an area on the east coast of England which is famous for its natural beauty and impressive architecture. Norwich is a wonderful city to explore and is popular with tourists all year round.

Norwich is not a city of luxurious hotels but it has a good selection of reasonably priced places to stay in, both in the city centre and further out. The Beeches Hotel, for example, next to the cathedral, has a beautiful Victorian garden and has just over twenty double rooms. Comfortable accommodation costs £65 for two nights' bed and breakfast per person; weekend breaks from October to May cost £59 per person. Norwich is famous for its magnificent cathedral. The cathedral has a summer programme of music and events which is open to the general public. One event, *Fire from Heaven*, is a drama and musical performance with fireworks, a laser light show and a carnival with local people dressed in colourful costumes.

Norwich is also home to the Sainsbury Centre For The Visual Arts, a world-class collection of international art in a building at the University of East Anglia designed by Sir Norman Foster. This is well worth a visit and there is a lovely canteen with an excellent selection of hot and cold snacks. It also specializes in vegetarian food.

The city has a new professional theatre, the Playhouse, on the River Wensum. The city's annual international arts festival is from 10-20 October. Not on the classic tourist agenda but well worth a visit are the factory shoe shops in Norwich (for men, women and children). Here you can buy shoes for less than half the shop price.

Finally, if you fancy a complete break from the stresses of everyday life, you could hire a boat and spend a few days cruising along the rivers of the famous Norfolk Broads. The Broads have changed for the better in recent years. In our environmentally friendly age, the emphasis has moved towards the quiet enjoyment of nature and wildlife. You can hire a boat, big or small, for an hour or two or even up to a week or two. This makes a perfect day out or holiday for people of all ages.

PART 4 | Questions 21-25

Read the text and questions below. For each question, mark the letter next to the correct answer A, B, C or D.

"Mandy Jones - Holiday Company Manager"

I did a business administration degree at Bristol University and then worked for a credit card company for eight years. During this time, I was assistant marketing manager. I gained a lot of useful experience doing this job, but in 1997, I decided that I needed a change. I moved to Thomson Holidays where I have worked as a manager ever since. My main job is to think up new and interesting ideas for holidays.

When I'm working from my office in the UK, I arrive at 9 a.m. First I answer my e-mails, then plan the day. My role is to investigate new projects for Thomson Holidays in our Mediterranean resorts. I am responsible for thinking up ideas, developing them and evaluating their success.

We have lots of meetings in the office which involve the marketing department, holiday reps and people that we bring in from outside such as entertainment organisers. The aim is to develop an exciting idea into a realistic and workable project.

Once a month I spend a few days overseas checking possible resorts, meeting with reps to develop their roles and working out how events should be sold to the customer. I work with resort supervisors, use their local knowledge of bars and clubs for venues, talk through new ideas and find out how existing ones are working. I also meet holidaymakers.

I have to be very open-minded because ideas come from anywhere. I love my job because I get to travel and I am working on projects that really excite me.

21. **What is the writer's main purpose in writing the text?**
   A. To explain the best way to choose a holiday.
   B. To advise people on holiday resorts.
   C. To explain what her job involves.
   D. To show how stressful her job is.

22. **What do we learn about the writer in the first paragraph?**
   A. She learned a lot from her first job.
   B. She disliked her first job.
   C. She lost her first job.
   D. She worked in the administration department of Bristol University.

23. **The writer has to**
   A. send e-mails all day.
   B. find out if new ideas could actually work.
   C. entertain the holiday reps.
   D. spend all of her time having meetings in the office.

24. **What does she say about her job?**
   A. She never knows where or how a new idea might come to her.
   B. It makes her very popular with lots of people.
   C. She spends too much time in bars and clubs.
   D. She has a few problems with local people at the resorts.

25. **Which of the following is the best description of the writer?**
   A. A working woman who very much enjoys what she does for a living.
   B. The travel agent who is trying to get a promotion.
   C. A woman who spends a lot of time on holiday and has an easy life.
   D. A woman who makes a lot of money by going to clubs and bars.

PAPER 1 - READING

PART 5   Questions 26-35

Read the text below and choose the correct word for each space. For each question, choose the correct letter **A, B, C or D**.

Example answer:

0	A	B	C	D
	▬			

"Ask your pharmacist first"

Minor **(0)** *illnesses* have a nasty habit of striking **(26)**.. the wrong time, don't they? **(27)**.. you have a pile of things to do at work and even more on your plate at home, the last thing you want is a **(28)**.. throat or a tension headache to drag you down. **(29)**.. this summer, when you're feeling **(30)**.. the weather, remember that a visit to your **(31)**.. pharmacy **(32)**.. be a real bonus in helping you get the right remedy to ease your symptoms. But it's not **(33)**.. the medication that assists the cure - only at a pharmacy will you find expert **(34)**.. from a highly trained health professional. Just try asking a supermarket shelf what it **(35)**.. for family health problems!

0.	**A.** *illnesses*	**B.** symptoms	**C.** handicaps	**D.** addictions
26.	**A.** for	**B.** at	**C.** in	**D.** to
27.	**A.** However	**B.** Although	**C.** Despite	**D.** When
28.	**A.** cut	**B.** sore	**C.** hurt	**D.** injured
29.	**A.** So	**B.** Then	**C.** As	**D.** On
30.	**A.** over	**B.** under	**C.** beneath	**D.** below
31.	**A.** native	**B.** national	**C.** local	**D.** domestic
32.	**A.** must	**B.** ought	**C.** can	**D.** did
33.	**A.** just	**B.** then	**C.** since	**D.** as
34.	**A.** messages	**B.** preparation	**C.** therapy	**D.** advice
35.	**A.** recommends	**B.** commands	**C.** orders	**D.** wants

WRITING

PART 1 | **Questions 1-5**

Here are some sentences about sport. For each question, complete the second sentence so that it means the same as the first, **using no more than three words**. Write only the missing words.

Example: I prefer swimming to cycling.
I like swimming **more than** cycling.

1. If you don't practise every week, you won't be a stronger swimmer.

   You won't be a stronger swimmer unless ....*you practise*........... **every week.**

2. Why don't you join a swimming team?

   If I were you, ...*I would*............... **join a swimming team.**

3. You can play tennis both indoors and outdoors.

   Tennis can ....*be played*.......... **both indoors and outdoors.**

4. A lot of people play tennis at this club.

   There are a lot of people ....*who play*............... **tennis at this club.**

5. "I haven't got time to play tennis often", she said.

   She said that she ...*didn't have / hadn't got*.... **enough time to play tennis often.**

PAPER 1 - WRITING

PART 2 | Question 6

An English friend of yours called Anne sent you a birthday present, which you liked.
Write a card to Anne. In your card, you should

- Thank her for the present.
- Say why you liked it.
- Tell her about one other present that you got for your birthday.

Write **35-45** words.

PART 3 | Question 7-8

Answer **ONE** of the following questions (**7 or 8**). Write about **100** words. Put the question number at the top of your answer.

Question 7
This is part of a letter you receive from an English pen friend.

Don't forget to tell me about the area you live in and what you and your friends do in your free time.

- Write a letter to your pen friend.
- Write your **letter** in about 100 words.

Question 8
- Your English teacher has asked you to write a story.
- Your story must begin with this sentence:

I was worried about the journey.

- Write your **story** in about 100 words.

PAPER 2 LISTENING

PART 1 Questions 1-7

There are seven questions in this part. For each question there are three pictures and a short recording. Choose the correct picture and put a tick (✓) in the box below it.

Example: *Where did the woman leave her hat?*

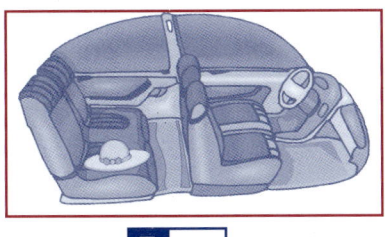

---

1. How did the woman travel?

2. What time does the film start?

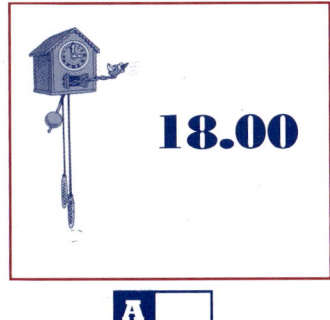

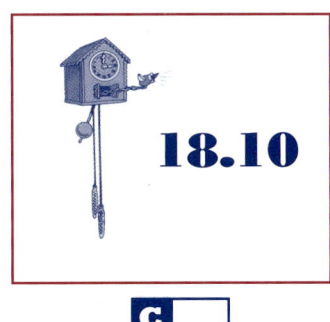

3. What does the man eat?

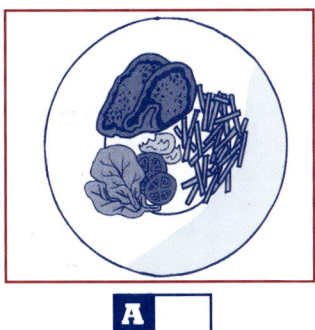

4. Which book is Jackie reading?

A ✓

B

C

5. Where did the man leave his keys?

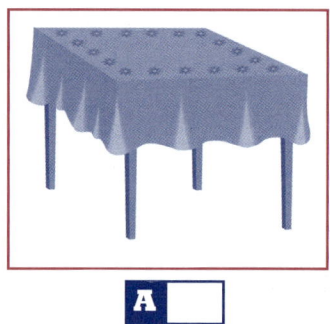

A

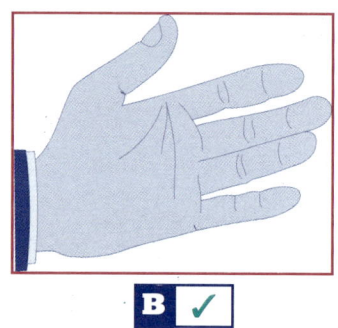

B ✓

C

6. Which present did Mark buy?

A ✓

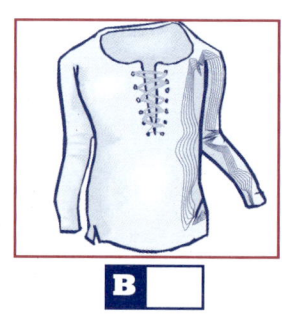

B

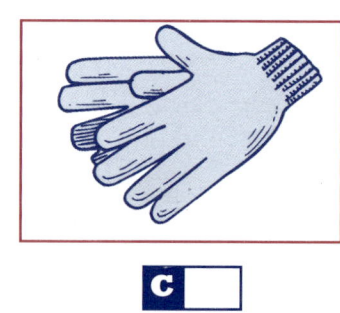

C

7. What will the weather be like tomorrow?

A ✓

B

C

PART 2 | Questions 8-13

You will hear a doctor talking about how people can lead a healthier life. For each question, put a tick (✓) in the correct box.

8. To become healthier you should

    A. dramatically change your life.

    B. change some daily habits.

    C. eat hardly anything.

A	
B	✓
C	

9. If you don't manage to exercise as much as you should

    A. leave the gym.

    B. try not to be negative about it.

    C. be angry with yourself.

A	
B	✓
C	

10. To improve your mood you should

    A. drink more tea and coffee.

    B. only eat vegetables.

    C. increase the amount of vegetables you eat.

A	
B	
C	✓

11. The survey

    A. showed quite dramatic results.

    B. didn't have strong results.

    C. didn't give any useful information.

A	✓
B	
C	

12. You should always

    A. do important jobs first.

    B. do everything as quickly as possible.

    C. try to finish what you start.

A	
B	
C	✓

13. The doctor says

    A. you should never have a late night.

    B. lack of sleep causes brain disease.

    C. it's okay to go to bed late sometimes.

A	
B	
C	✓

PAPER 2 – LISTENING

You will hear a tour guide giving information about an old British house. For each question, fill in the missing information in the numbered space.

The house was built in the (14) .... 19th century ....

The Reynold family lived in the house until (15) .... 1975 ....

The servants had rooms in the (16) .... attic ....

The art collection is in the (17) .... dining room ....

George Reynold was a (18) .... lawyer ....

George's brother died in a (19) .... horse riding .... accident.

Look at the six sentences for this part. You will hear a conversation between a boy, Simon, and a girl, Tina, about some problems Tina is having at school. Decide if each sentence is correct or incorrect. If it is correct, put a tick (✓) in the box under **A for YES**. If it is not correct, put a tick (✓) in the box under **B for NO**.

	A YES	B NO
20. Simon thinks Tina should talk about her problems.	✓	
21. Simon agrees that the teachers are unfair.		✓
22. Tina doesn't concentrate in class.	✓	
23. Tina is ill.		✓
24. Simon feels sorry for Tina.		✓
25. Tina realises her mistake.	✓	

Test 2

PAPER 1 READING & WRITING

PART 1 Questions 1-5

Look at the text in each question. What does it say? Mark the letter next to the correct explanation **A, B** or **C**.

Example:

0

> **NO BALL GAMES ALLOWED ON THE GRASS**

A. You may not sit on the grass.
B. Be careful not to damage the grass while playing ball games on it.
C. All ball games are forbidden on the grass.

Example answer: | **0** | *C* |

1

> **MESSAGE**
> Tony - the bookshop phoned to say they've got the book you ordered. They will keep it until Friday and then it will go out on the shelves.

A. The shop will have Tony's book by Friday.
B. Tony needs to collect the book by Friday.
C. The book is being delivered on Friday.

2

> **CUSTOMER NOTICE**
> The store will close at 4pm on Wednesday for a stock check. Normal opening hours of 9-5 will resume on Thursday.

A. The store will open later than normal on Wednesday.
B. The store usually closes at 4pm.
C. On Wednesday the store will close an hour earlier than usual.

3

> Please return all books by the due back date. There will be a fine for overdue books. Books may be renewed over the telephone on the condition that they have not been reserved by another borrower.

A. All books must be renewed by telephone.
B. All books must be reserved by borrowers.
C. Books must be returned on time.

4

> Please leave any parcels with number 24, Monday to Friday. No junk mail please.

A. All post should be taken to number 24.
B. Junk mail should not be posted here.
C. No mail is accepted at weekends.

5

> **To:** Mick
> **From:** Sharon
> **Re:** lecture notes
> Hi Mick, can you e-mail me the history notes from Monday afternoon's lecture? I was under the weather and missed it. See you at the theatre Friday, Sharon

A. Sharon was too ill to go to the lecture.
B. Bad weather prevented Sharon from going to the lecture.
C. Sharon went to the theatre instead of the lecture.

PART 2 | **Questions 6-10**

These people (6-10) all want to do a part-time course at college. Look at the eight reviews (A-H). Decide which course would be the most suitable for each person. For questions 6-10, choose the correct letter (**A-H**).

6. Jack is eighteen. He works in a supermarket but he'd really like to get a job in a bank. He did well in his exams at school but he'd like to do a course that will help him get a better job.

6 | G

7. Cathy is a police officer. She would like to do something relaxing that will take her mind off her work. She would enjoy doing something creative but without having to use her brain too much.

7 | D

8. Daniel is 36 years old and works in Information Technology. He spends all day sitting at a computer and is putting on a lot of weight. He'd also like to do a course that is quite sociable in order to meet new people.

8 | B

9. Debbie is 29 years old. She is a housewife and has two young children who have just started school. She regrets not going to college and hopes to get a job when her children are older. Ideally, she would like to work with children.

9 | E

10. Rupert is 68 years old. He has retired but he used to be an architect. He has just bought a cottage in the countryside which he is slowly renovating because it is in bad condition. He enjoys walking and being outside in the fresh air.

10 | C

College Courses

A. Chess for beginners

A great pastime for all ages. Come and exercise your mind and make new friends at the same time. Learn from an ex British chess champion who has played against some of the great Russian players. Classes every Monday evening from 7-9 p.m., or Wednesday morning 9.30-11.30 a.m.

B. Basketball (for men and women)

Come and have a great workout as well as a lot of fun. We offer beginners and improvers classes. Experienced instructors. Join the college team and take part in weekend league competitions. Transport provided, free of charge, to games.
Tues/Thurs Evening 7-9 p.m.
League Matches, Sunday afternoons.

C. Gardening

Transform your garden into a paradise to be proud of. This course is run by two lecturers. One is a garden designer and the other is a horticulturist. This means that you will not only learn how to grow plants but you will also learn which plants go well together, both aesthetically and naturally. You will be the envy of all of your neighbours.
Mon and Fri 9 a.m. - 12 p.m.

D. Fine Art

This course will give you a taste of drawing, painting, sculpture and even pottery. You will be given basic guidance and then encouraged to develop your own ideas and creative skills. All materials are provided as part of the course although students may wish to buy a small portfolio to carry their work to and from college.
Tues and Friday mornings 10 a.m. - 1 p.m.

E. Becoming a Teaching Assistant

Although this course doesn't lead to a formal qualification, it will prepare you for many aspects of life in the classroom. You will learn about teaching basic reading, writing and mathematics at primary level, that is ages 4 to 11. You will get to spend some mornings in a local primary school, working alongside experienced, qualified teachers. This is a good foundation for those wishing to take an NVQ in education.

F. Basic car maintenance

Learn how to fix small problems on your car. Basics such as checking the oil, changing a tyre, jump starting a flat battery and changing a blown bulb are all covered. You will also learn how to detect potential problems such as fan belt or brake pad problems. Make your car safer and save yourself money by doing this highly practical course.
Weds and Fri afternoons 3-6 p.m.

G. Basic Computing

This course starts at two levels. The first is for absolute beginners who have never used a computer and the second level is for people who have a very basic knowledge of computers but want to develop their skills for home, study or work reasons.
There will be a specific emphasis on using the Internet to its full potential and how to avoid problems with the Internet.
Monday and Wednesday evenings 7-10 p.m.

H. Creative Writing

Find the poet or novelist hidden deep inside you. In this course you will be taught by a published poet and a published author. They will offer you guidelines on how to improve and develop your writing skills as well as tips on how to approach publishers or agents. This is a fairly intense course which demands a lot of work to be completed at home.
Mon, Weds, Thurs afternoons 2-5 p.m.

PART 3 | Questions 11-20

Look at the sentences below about a safety leaflet. Read the text to decide if each sentence is correct or incorrect. If it is correct, mark **A**. If it is not correct, mark **B**.

11. If there is a fire, leave the house and then shout.	11	B
12. If the smoke alarm sounds, sit down and make an escape plan.	12	B
13. You should decide what you would do before a fire starts.	13	A
14. Smoke rises in a room.	14	A
15. Jump out of a window arms first.	15	B
16. You should have an alarm in each room.	16	B
17. Don't smoke at night in your house.	17	B
18. Make sure that everyone is aware of the escape route.	18	A
19. If you are trapped, stay by a window.	19	A
20. Never return to a burning building.	20	A

What to do if there's a fire

Raise the alarm
- If your smoke alarm goes off while you are asleep, don't investigate to see if there is a fire. Shout to wake everyone up, get everyone together, follow your plan and get out.
- Check doors with the back of your hand - if they are warm, do not open them - the fire is on the other side.
- If there is a lot of smoke, crawl along with your nose near the floor where the air will be cleaner.

Escaping from a window
- If you are on the ground floor or first floor you may be able to escape from a window. If you have to break the window, cover the jagged glass with towels or thick bedding.
- Throw some more bedding out of the window to break your fall. Don't jump out of the window - lower yourself down to arm's length and drop to the ground.
- If you have any children or elderly or disabled people with you, plan the order you will escape in so that you can help them down.

Don't go back inside your home
- Call the Fire Brigade from a mobile phone, a neighbour's house or a phone box. Give the address of the fire.
- Don't stop or go back for anything.

Practise your fire action plan
- Knowing what to do and acting quickly will save lives. Regularly take a few minutes to "walk" the escape route with everyone in your household and check that everyone

can unlock and open windows and doors easily.
- Review your plan regularly, especially if you make any changes in your home.
- Protect yourself and reduce the risk of fire by:
- Fitting smoke alarms on each floor level and testing them each week.
- Keeping doors closed at night.
- Switching off as many electrical appliances as possible at night.
- Putting out cigarettes and candles safely and keeping matches and lighters away from children.

What to do if your escape route is blocked
- Get everyone into one room and close the door. Smoke and fumes can kill people quickly, so put bedding or towels along the bottom of the door to seal the gap.
- Open the window and stay near it for fresh air and to let the firefighters see you.
- Phone the Fire Brigade or shout for help so that someone else can phone for you.

In summary, to save your life in a fire:
- if your smoke alarm goes off in the night don't investigate
- wake others and get out, following your plan;
- don't open any doors that feel warm;
- don't stop or go back for anything - phone the Fire Brigade; and
- if you can't get out, stay together in one room, close the door and wait to be rescued.

PAPER 1 - READING

Read the text and questions below. For each question, choose the correct letter **A, B, C** or **D**.

There can be something brutal about emerging pale and tired from an overnight flight into the bright African sun. However, when you are met by a smiling, tanned pilot who whisks you through Customs and on to the runway to a waiting plane, life suddenly seems a whole lot better. When you are on a short break every hour matters so we were short-cutting the queues at Customs and heading off to the bush in time for breakfast.

The flight north from Nairobi lasts less than an hour but is a fascinating safari in itself. It took us out of the city and low over the patchwork fields and dark red roads of the Kenyan agricultural heartland until we reached Mount Kenya. Here suddenly the view changes. The pilot swooped breathtakingly low over the trees pointing out the elephants, giraffes, gazelles and even rhinos as they scattered beneath us. The tiny shadow of the plane followed us across the dry rugged land. We circled high above our final destination, Loisaba Lodge, before landing neatly on the dirt airstrip.

Loisaba Wilderness is a 150sq km, privately managed wildlife conservancy. It is larger than many of Kenya's game parks and a haven for more than 250 species of bird and 50 species of mammal - elephants, buffaloes. The wildlife here, unlike in the game parks, is still wild, and so, far more exciting to see than bored lions sprawled in front of a crowd of tourists in jeeps.

The lodge perches high on a ridge. From each of the seven rooms guests can walk out on to their private terrace to marvel at the wildly dramatic view - 61,000 acres of acacia savannah and rocky outcrops lie beneath you.

A thousand feet straight down the escarpment is a watering hole constantly drawing in animals for a drink; shimmering in the far distance swathed in cloud sit the darkly forested foothills of Mount Kenya. It's a view to knock you out, to savour, to return to again and again.

21. **Why has the writer written this piece?**
   A. to warn people about the dangers of a trip to Africa
   B. to inform people about a short break in Africa
   C. to discuss endangered species in Africa
   D. to make people more aware of animal conservation

22. **Why was the writer so pleased to be met by the pilot?**
   A. Because he wanted to make the most of his time on holiday.
   B. Because he thought the pilot might not meet him.
   C. Because he expected the pilot to be unfriendly.
   D. Because the pilot showed him how to push up in the queue without being noticed.

23. **What does the writer say about the flight from Nairobi?**
   A. It is far too short.
   B. The pilot flew in a dangerous way.
   C. They were followed by a smaller plane.
   D. It offers many impressive views.

24. **What does the writer suggest about Loisaba?**
   A. It is still a safe and natural environment for animals.
   B. Tourists are spoiling it.
   C. Many of the animals are being hunted.
   D. The wild animals often attack people.

25. **Which of the following would be the best title for this text?**
   A. "Wild animals in danger"
   B. "A taste of natural Africa"
   C. "A day trip to the zoo"
   D. "Tourists are taking over beautiful Africa"

PART 5 Questions 26-35

Read the text below and choose the correct word for each space. For each question, choose the correct letter **A, B, C** *or* **D.**

Example: **0** A B C D (D marked)

If you had asked Ann a few years **(0)** ***ago*** what she would be doing in five years' **(26)**................................, she wouldn't have believed you if you had suggested she would be cabin crew. Likewise, when she told her friends that she had **(27)**.................................... for a job, most of them laughed. **(28)**..............................., after successfully completing her four week cabin crew training **(29)**.................................. and embarking **(30)**.................................. a new career, the only person laughing now is Ann! **(31)**................................. many cabin crew, Ann has had to make some changes in **(32)**.................................. to meet the demands of her new career. She is expected to work at any time of the day on any day of the year, and sometimes operates up to six flights per day. The days can be long and the work tiring, but Ann is enjoying the unique and **(33)**.................................. lifestyle that being cabin crew brings.

In return for her hard work, Ann can enjoy a **(34)**...................................... of up to 17,000 pounds (or 20,000 pounds for a senior cabin crew member), staff travel concessions and 36 days annual leave. Easy Jet cabin crew also have the privilege of working on some of the newest aircraft in Europe and can experience fast track promotions.

If you would like to **(35)**.................................... in Ann's footsteps, and be considered as cabin crew at London Luton, London Gatwick or London Stansted, please visit our website for more information and to complete an online application form.

0.	**A.** by	**B.** since	**C.** later	**D.** ***ago***
26.	**A.** time	**B.** later	**C.** next	**D.** future
27.	**A.** appealed	**B.** applied	**C.** assigned	**D.** requested
28.	**A.** Moreover	**B.** Despite	**C.** However	**D.** Because
29.	**A.** route	**B.** sequence	**C.** course	**D.** track
30.	**A.** on	**B.** for	**C.** at	**D.** to
31.	**A.** Like	**B.** With	**C.** Also	**D.** Plus
32.	**A.** deed	**B.** order	**C.** need	**D.** particular
33.	**A.** disturbing	**B.** challenging	**C.** reforming	**D.** unreliable
34.	**A.** fee	**B.** compensation	**C.** bill	**D.** salary
35.	**A.** step	**B.** accompany	**C.** chase	**D.** follow

WRITING

PART 1 Questions 1-5

Here are some sentences about work and employment. For each question, complete the second sentence so that it means the same as the first, <u>using no more than three words</u>. Write only the missing words.

> **Example:** **(0)** *I'd sooner be a teacher than a doctor.*
> *I'd prefer **to be** a teacher than a doctor.*

---

1. It is easier to work in a relaxed office than a stressful one.

   ....*Working*..................... **in a relaxed office is easier than working in a stressful one.**

2. Why doesn't she apply for a new job?

   If I were her ....*I would apply*................. **for a new job.**

3. The last time I had a business meeting with him was in February.

   I haven't had a business meeting with him ....*since*................. **February.**

4. When I first started this job I often made a lot of mistakes.

   I ....*used to*................. **make a lot of mistakes when I first started this job.**

5. After watching a documentary about studying abroad, Sheila decided to study in England.

   Sheila ....*watched /had watched*............ **a documentary and then decided to study in England.**

PART 2 | Question 6

You want to invite an English friend of yours to come and stay with you in the summer.
Write a card to your friend. In your card, you should

- Invite your friend.
- Tell him/her something about the place where you live.
- Suggest a good time for him/her to come.

Write **35-45** words.

PART 3 | Question 7-8

Write an answer to **ONE** of the questions (**7 or 8**) in this part. Write your answer in about **100** words. Put the question number at the top of your answer.

Question 7

This is part of a letter you receive from an English pen friend.

> In your next letter, please tell me about a popular holiday destination in your country. What can you do and see there? Is it a good place for young people to visit?

Now write a **letter** answering your pen friend's questions.

Question 8

- Your English teacher has asked you to write a story.
- Your story must begin with this sentence:

  I took a deep breath and knocked on the door.

- Write your **story**.

PAPER 2   LISTENING

PART 1   Questions 1-7

There are seven questions in this part. For each question there are three pictures and a short recording. Choose the correct picture and put a tick (✓) in the box below it.

Example: *Where did the woman leave her hat?*

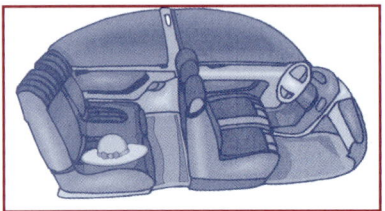  

A   **B** ✓   **C**

---

1. How did the man get to work?

A ✓   **B**   **C**

2. What does the woman buy?

  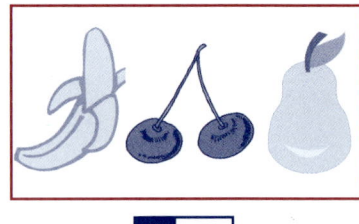

A   **B**   **C** ✓

3. What kind of film was it?

Adventure   Sad Romance

A   **B** ✓   **C**

4. What will Ben do Saturday afternoon?

A [ ]

B [ ]

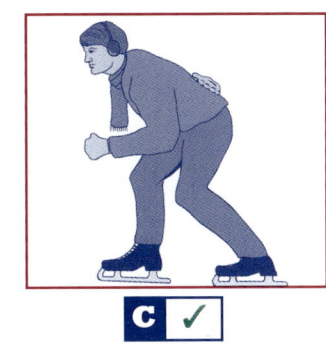

C [✓]

5. What did Alison do?

A [✓]

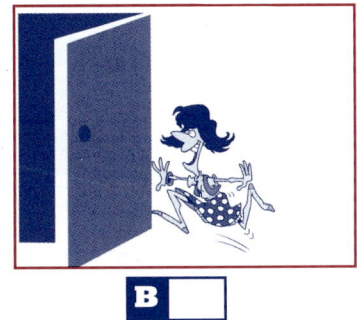

B [ ]

C [ ]

6. What animal will they buy?

A [ ]

B [✓]

C [ ]

7. What time will Sue collect the children?

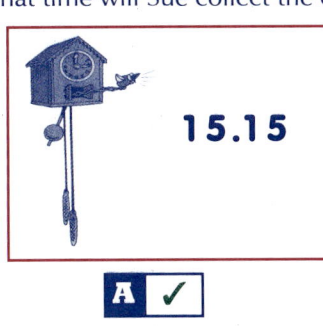

15.15

A [✓]

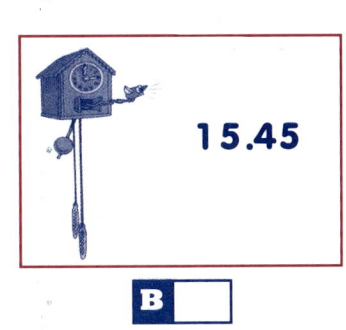

15.45

B [ ]

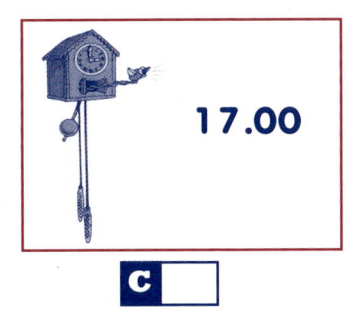

17.00

C [ ]

PAPER 2 - LISTENING

PART 2   Questions 8-13

You will hear a man called Ian talking on the radio about difficult neighbours. For each question, put a tick (✓) in the correct box.

8. **Why couldn't Isabel sleep?**

   A. Her flatmate was too noisy.

   B. The phone kept ringing.

   C. The downstairs neighbour was shouting.

A	
B	
C	✓

9. **Isabel was angry because**

   A. this had happened many times before.

   B. the man was shouting at her.

   C. people were phoning her late at night.

A	✓
B	
C	

10. **What happened when Isabel approached the man?**

    A. He hit her.

    B. He reluctantly apologised.

    C. He wasn't at all sorry.

    | A | |
    | B | |
    | C | ✓ |

11. **Why did Isabel move?**

    A. The man followed her home from work.

    B. Nobody would do anything about the man.

    C. The renting agency asked her to.

    | A | |
    | B | ✓ |
    | C | |

12. **According to research**

    A. one in ten people argue with their neighbours.

    B. one in ten people are disturbed by noise.

    C. one in ten people are forced to move home.

    | A | |
    | B | ✓ |
    | C | |

13. **According to Lisa Dorn**

    A. modern living conditions cause problems.

    B. people no longer know their neighbours.

    C. people are more lonely than they used to be.

    | A | ✓ |
    | B | |
    | C | |

PART 3 **Questions 14-19**

You will hear a tour guide talking to a group of people. For each question, fill in the missing information in the numbered space.

Excursion to Brighton
ITINERARY

COACH PICK UP TIME: 8 a.m.
PICK UP POINT: outside the **(14)** .... Town Hall ....
ARRIVAL TIME IN BRIGHTON: 10 a.m.
DROP OFF POINT: POOL VALLEY COACH station

GUIDED WALKING TOUR

10.15 - 10.45: Tour of the famous Brighton Lanes (Famous for **(15)** .... jewellers .... and boutiques).

11am - 12.30pm: Coffee break. Refreshments are available inside the Palace cafe
or in the **(16)** .... Pavilion Gardens .... cafe.

11.30 - 12.30: Guided tour of the palace.

12.45 - 2pm: Lunch at Donatello Restaurant.
Two-course lunch **(17)** .... £6.95 ....
Three-course lunch **£**8.95
Coffee/tea included

2pm - 3pm: Brighton Museum and Art Gallery.
Guided tour optional - free of charge.

3pm - 5pm: Free time on Brighton seafront.
Recommended sights: Brighton Pier, **(18)** .... Aquarium .... and artists' studios.

5.10 - 6pm: Grand Hotel for **(19)** .... cream tea ....
Depart from Pool Valley Coach Station.

PART 4 **Questions 20-25**

*Look at the six sentences for this part. You will hear a conversation between a man, Simon, and a woman, Samantha, about London. Decide if each sentence is correct or incorrect. If it is correct, put a tick (✓) in the box under **A for YES**. If it is not correct, put a tick (✓) in the box under **B for NO**.*

		A YES	B NO
20.	Samantha thought the art in Tate Modern was impressive.		✓
21.	Simon didn't want to go on the London Eye.		✓
22.	Simon thought the Chinese food was value for money.	✓	
23.	The popular theatre shows are always expensive.		✓
24.	Samantha often goes to concerts.		✓
25.	Samantha felt uncomfortable on public transport.	✓	

Test 3

PAPER 1 READING & WRITING

PART 1 Questions 1-5

Look at the text in each question. What does it say? Mark the letter next to the correct explanation **A, B** or **C**.

Example:

0

> **NO BALL GAMES ALLOWED ON THE GRASS**

A. You may not sit on the grass.
B. Be careful not to damage the grass while playing ball games on it.
C. All ball games are forbidden on the grass.

Example answer:  0 C

1

> **NOTE**
> Tim, Could you do the dishes and walk Scooby? I'll be back at 6.
> Love Mum

 C

A. Tim's mum has taken the dog for a walk.
B. Tim must cook the dinner.
C. Tim must walk the dog and clean the plates.

2

> E-mail
> To: Maria From: James
> This week I'm going to visit Dover; it'll make a nice change from rainy Glasgow. Maybe we could meet?

 C

A. James lives in Dover.
B. James is going to visit Glasgow.
C. Maria lives in Dover.

3

> **NOTICE**
> On Saturday 16th of October trials will take place for the 1st and 2nd football teams. All those wishing to enter should give their name and class to Mr. Johnson.

 B

A. The first school football match will take place on Saturday.
B. The football teams will be chosen from how well people play on Saturday.
C. Everyone must go to the football trials on Saturday the 16th.

4

> **LABEL**
> Take one pill three times a day until the course is finished. If you have any side-effects such as headaches, stomachaches or nausea, stop taking your medication and call your doctor immediately.

 A

A. You must take all the pills unless they make you ill.
B. You must take a pill every three days unless they make you ill.
C. You should call your doctor when you finish the pills.

5

> **SIGN**
> DROPPING LITTER IN THE PARK IS AN OFFENCE. USE THE RUBBISH BINS PROVIDED. ANYONE CAUGHT DROPPING LITTER CAN BE FINED UP TO £100.

 B

A. You can only drop litter near the park bins.
B. If you are caught dropping litter you might have to pay a fine.
C. If you cannot find a bin, you can drop rubbish in the park.

PART 2 | Questions 6-10

These people (6-10) all want to choose a hotel to stay in for the weekend. Look at the eight reviews (A-H). Decide which hotel would be the most suitable for each person. For questions 6-10, choose the correct letter (A-H).

6. Anthony Bitters is a businessman who is travelling to different cities in England over the weekend. He needs to be near major roads and transport centres to go to meetings. He also needs to be in constant contact with his offices and the latest business news.

6	B

7. John and Alex like outdoor activities and adventure weekends. They want to stay somewhere organised where they can sleep in their tents and be close to nature, but are not worried about comfort or luxury.

7	D

8. The Peterson family are travelling from the south of England to Scotland in the north, with their two children. They need a suitable hotel for just one night, which should be simple and near to the motorway.

8	G

9. Stephanie and Sophie want to go walking and exploring the countryside, and need only a clean simple place to sleep, as they will be out all day. They do not like camping.

9	A

10. George and Maria are celebrating their two-year wedding anniversary, and want to spend a romantic and luxurious weekend away from the city. It is important that they relax and are away from noise and stress.

10	E

Accommodation Options

A. The Countryside Inn
This tidy, traditional bed and breakfast hotel is located in the village of Minton in the heart of the beautiful Chilton hills. Single and double rooms are available at reasonable prices with breakfast included, perfect for those wanting to enjoy the local scenery.

B. The Corporate
The new extremely comfortable corporate hotel is located halfway between Birmingham and London, and is only half a mile from the M40 motorway and allows you to reach whatever city you require in England. There are single or double rooms with 'office features' such as Internet and two phone line connections in each room, as well as satellite TV included in the price.

C. The Drive-by
For busy travellers arriving from Europe this small hotel in the middle of the town of Dover, Southeast England, provides reasonably priced single and double rooms without the need to reserve. Ideal rest for sleepy travellers.

D. Peak Campsite
Located at the edge of the Lake District National Park with its spectacular mountain ranges and lakes, this is a basic but well managed campsite. There is a shower and toilet building, but you have to bring your own tent and equipment.

E. Hotel Amour
Located on a peaceful seafront on the South coast, with spectacular sunset views, the Hotel Amour is ideal for honeymoons or couples who want a personal break from the stress of life. Each double room or honeymoon suite is expensively decorated for your comfort and includes a free bottle of champagne on your first night.

F. Buffalo Bill's Ranch
Wild-west theme hotel in the Southwest countryside, ideal for a week away with the children. You can stay on a re-creation of a 19th century American farm, ride horses with real cowboys and be served by Native American Indians at dinner.

G. Travellers' Lodge
Conveniently located in the middle of the country, just half a mile form the north-south M1 motorway. Ideal for those making the long trip up or down the country. Simple rooms and reasonable prices for single, or double rooms, with a fifty percent discount for kids and breakfast included.

H. Hotel Royal
Luxury in the heart of the city, good enough for a King, and located near the lively West End theatre and shopping district. Each room (whether single, double or honeymoon suite) has an en-suite sauna. Treat yourself to a weekend in style.

PART 3 Questions 11-20

Look at the sentences below about 'Richardson's pubs'. Read the text to decide if each sentence is correct or incorrect. If it is correct, mark **A**. If it is not correct, mark **B**.

11. Richardson's pubs were renovated and improved not very long ago.

| 11 | A |

12. Many of the pubs have their own tales and legends.

| 12 | A |

13. The pubs do not serve both food and drink.

| 13 | B |

14. Service is not very important at Richardson's pubs.

| 14 | B |

15. The people who work at Richardson's pubs are pleased to take care of you.

| 15 | A |

16. You shouldn't ask the staff if you need anything.

| 16 | B |

17. At Richardson's pubs you can eat or drink whenever you'd like to.

| 17 | A |

18. These pubs are quieter than most bars usually are.

| 18 | A |

19. Richardson's pubs have only traditional, local drinks.

| 19 | B |

20. Sometimes there are special, extra drinks available.

| 20 | A |

Richardson's Pubs

The new look.
You are always welcome at a Richardson's pub, all of which we have recently, carefully restored to look as good as possible. As you can see when you take a look around, we're extremely proud of our heritage. Our pubs are traditional, cosy and, we think, "good old-fashioned" places to enjoy a well-kept pint of beer, or a glass of something refreshing, or even a tasty bite to eat. Many of our pubs have a history that can be traced back over centuries. Every pub will have a story or two to tell! Our bar staff may be able to tell you more. So, whether you're popping in for a quick drink, a meal, or if you're here for a good night out, enjoy yourself.

The service.
Now there's a word that doesn't mean quite what it used to. But at Richardson's we try as hard as we can to deliver individual, high standards of service that you'll want to come back to and experience again. At the heart of our pubs is friendly, helpful staff that enjoy looking after you. If there's anything we can do to make your visit more enjoyable, please don't hesitate to ask. We hope we'll be seeing you regularly.

The relaxed atmosphere.
What do you look for in a pub? A comfortable corner to enjoy a meal and a chat? A place at the bar to drink and get involved in a lively conversation? Or perhaps a seat in a window to read or quietly watch the world go by as you sip slowly at your glass. Whichever - and whenever you pop in - we're certain you'll find yourself at home in a Richardson's pub.
Relaxing, welcoming, it's a long way from the hustle and bustle of the typical bar. You may even find your watch ticks a little slower. So, enjoy the atmosphere, it's free.

Our selection of speciality beers and wines.
Our pubs may have the feel of a traditional local, but our selection of beers and wines is truly international. From real ales hand-pulled from the cask, to wines drawn from some of the most notable vineyards around the world.
Make no mistake, our cellar men and our vintners are proud of both the quality and variety of the beers and wines they bring you and the way they are expertly kept. As well as our regular selection, keep your eyes open for guest ales and special wines that they may find for you.

The delicious new buffet menu.
At Richardson's we don't just serve food as an after-thought, our kitchen is as important as our bar, and it shows in our great buffet menu.

PART 4 | Questions 21-25

Read the text and questions below. For each question, choose the correct letter **A, B, C** or **D.**

Tom Cruise

Over the years, Tom Cruise has become one of the most popular and successful actors in the world. Tom is now an international star, who gets paid millions of dollars for every film he makes. "I'm lucky," says Tom. "I'm doing what I love, and I'm having a great time. Lots of people would love to do this job, but they didn't get the lucky breaks or chances that I did." For many of us however, Tom was more than just lucky or good-looking, as acting ability and great determination were needed for him to become one of Hollywood's biggest names.

Is Tom happy with his success so far? He has a different outlook on his career than you might expect, "I've always looked to the future," says Tom. "I feel I'm always developing as an actor. I'm looking for new things all the time. I want to challenge myself to be better and always try new things. I know I've made a lot of progress in my career, but I still have ambitions for the future."

After interviewing him, I understood that the real Tom Cruise is a man with a very interesting and agreeable personality. He has a mind of his own and he's not like the characters in his movies, even though they may reflect Tom's personal style in the way he plays them.

The amazing success of Tom's career has been due to his talent as an actor and his personal strength and single-mindedness. Tom knew what he wanted to do with his life and gave his best to succeed.

21. **The purpose of this text is to**
   A. discuss Tom Cruise's success in acting.
   B. promote Tom Cruise's latest film.
   C. tell the story of Tom Cruise's childhood.
   D. negatively criticise Tom Cruise.

22. **What does Tom say about other people who try to become actors?**
   A. They are not as hard working as successful actors.
   B. He was more fortunate at certain points in his career.
   C. They did not love the job as much as he did.
   D. He took more risks to achieve success.

23. **How does Tom describe his attitude to his work?**
   A. He is only interested in making millions of dollars as an international star.
   B. He is unlucky and has had many breaks in his career.
   C. He looks forward and wants to improve and develop.
   D. He is determined to become famous one day, whatever the cost.

24. **The writer says that Tom Cruise**
   A. hides his real personality.
   B. has a personality similar to the characters he plays.
   C. has no personal style when acting.
   D. is very likeable as a person.

25. **How might the author describe Tom Cruise's success?**
   A. "A combination of luck and connections."
   B. "Something everyone can achieve."
   C. "A result of hard work and willpower."
   D. "Unfinished and incomplete."

PART 5   **Questions 26-35**

Read the text below and choose the correct word for each space. For each question, choose the correct letter **A, B, C** *or* **D.**

Example: | 0 | A   B   C   D |

Denmark

Denmark is the **(0)*smallest*** and most southerly of the countries of Scandinavia, **(26)**........................... lie in northern Europe. It is probably best **(27)**.............. for being home to the powerful Vikings, **(28)**...................... 1,000 years ago. Denmark is a small country, with limited natural **(29)**.............. . Nevertheless, it has become one of the richest countries in the **(30)**.............. .

Denmark has its own **(31)**.............. culture and traditions, and a tongue-twisting language, which includes several different dialects. Although Denmark is a member **(32)**.............. the European Union, recently it has been reluctant to work more closely with the EU and give up **(33)**.............. of its independence.

Wealth in Denmark is shared out more evenly than in most countries, because people pay high taxes. Many workers pay more than 50 percent of their wages in tax. The money is used to pay **(34)**.............. a welfare system, which includes health care, benefits for the unemployed and the elderly, and public services. Compared to the rest of the world, it is **(35)**.............. to become either very rich or very poor in Denmark.

0.	**A. *smallest***	**B.** highest	**C.** tallest	**D.** biggest
26.	**A.** whose	**B.** when	**C. which**	**D.** where
27.	**A.** liked	**B. known**	**C.** seen	**D.** heard
28.	**A. over**	**B.** more	**C.** since	**D.** less
29.	**A. resources**	**B.** features	**C.** natures	**D.** sources
30.	**A.** earth	**B.** land	**C.** space	**D. world**
31.	**A.** distant	**B. distinctive**	**C.** disliked	**D.** disinterested
32.	**A.** from	**B.** to	**C.** in	**D. of**
33.	**A.** many	**B.** every	**C.** very	**D. some**
34.	**A.** at	**B. for**	**C.** on	**D.** to
35.	**A.** impossible	**B.** simple	**C. difficult**	**D.** easy

WRITING

PART 1 **Questions 1-5**

Here are some sentences about playing football. For each question, complete the second sentence so that it means the same as the first, **using no more than three words**. Write only the missing words.

Example: **(0)** She has never liked to watch football.
She has always **disliked watching** football.

---

1. It is three years since Mike and I went to the stadium for the last time.

   Mike and I .... *have not been* .... **to the stadium for three years.**

2. Buy a season ticket, and you can go to the match every week.

   If you had a season ticket, ... *you would/could go* .... **to the match every week.**

3. The manager bought three new players last year.

   Three new players .... *were bought by* .... **the manager last year.**

4. The team scored too few goals and didn't win its last game.

   The team did not score .... *enough goals* .... **to win its last game.**

5. The young defender performed well in his first match.

   The young defender gave a good .... *performance* .... **in his first match.**

PAPER 1 - WRITING

PART 2 | Question 6

Your English friend Jim has shown you around the famous sights of London.
Write a card to Jim. In your card you should

- Thank him for showing you the city.
- Say what you enjoyed seeing most.
- Invite Jim to visit you.

Write **35-45** words.

PART 3 | Question 7-8

Write an answer to **ONE** of the questions (**7 or 8**) in this part. Write your answer in about **100** words. Put the question number at the top of your answer.

Question 7
This is part of a letter you receive from an English pen friend.

> In your next letter tell me about your favourite meal.
> What ingredients is it made of? How often do you eat it?

Now write a **letter** answering his/her questions.

Question 8

- Your English teacher has asked you to write a story.
- Your story must begin with this sentence.

    It started to rain heavily.

- Write your **story**.

PAPER 2   LISTENING

PART 1   Questions 1-7

There are seven questions in this part. For each question there are three pictures and a short recording. Choose the correct picture and put a tick (✓) in the box below it.

Example: *Where did the woman leave her hat?*

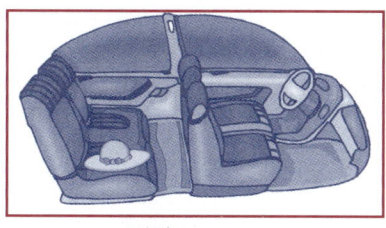

1. What is the weather like in Sydney?

2. How did the woman learn about the accident?

3. What will they eat at the restaurant?

4. What did the man buy from the supermarket?

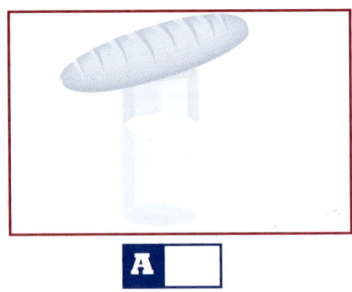

A ☐

B ✓

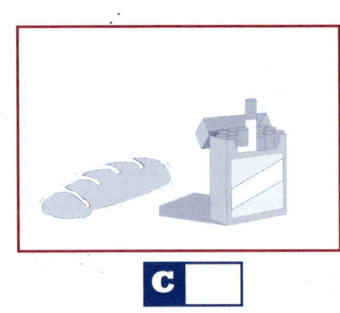

C ☐

5. How are tourists advised to travel?

A ☐

B ☐

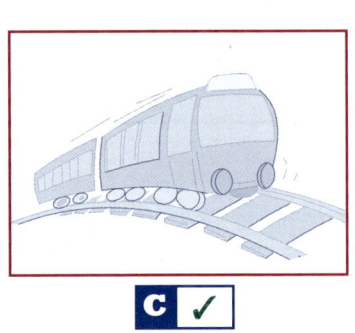

C ✓

6. On what date is the birthday party?

A ☐

B ✓

C ☐

7. Which instrument can Ben play?

A ✓

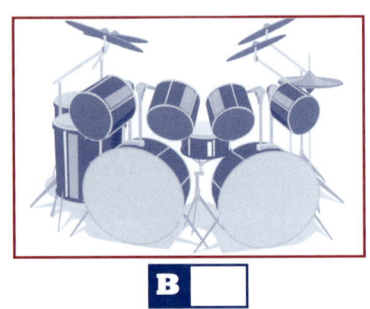

B ☐

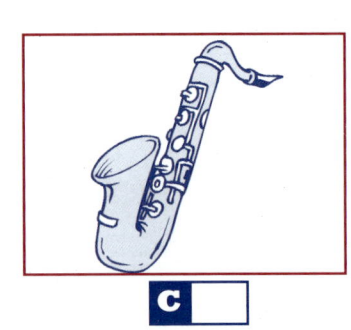

C ☐

PART 2 | Questions 8-13

You will hear a man describing a series of books. For each question, put a tick (✓) in the correct box.

8. Why does he like 'The Planet Wars'?

    A. It has a believable plot.   A ☐

    B. The story is fascinating.   B ✓

    C. The characters are deeply emotional.   C ☐

9. What is his problem with 'A Long Way Home'?

    A. It was too long.   A ✓

    B. The idea was bad.   B ☐

    C. The writing was bad.   C ☐

10. What does he say is original about 'Catch a Dream'?

    A. The happy ending.   A ☐

    B. The magical abilities of the characters.   B ☐

    C. The changing emotions of the characters.   C ✓

11. The horror story is about

    A. a war between humans and vampires.   A ☐

    B. Dracula trying to use science to take over the world.   B ☐

    C. a battle between two groups of vampires.   C ✓

12. What is not true about 'A World of Stories'?

    A. It is a collection of different children's stories.   A ☐

    B. Forty children from around the world tell their life stories.   B ✓

    C. Stories are included from different continents.   C ☐

13. What does he think about 'The Real Shakespeare'?

    A. It does not contain accurate facts.   A ✓

    B. It will be remembered as a classic.   B ☐

    C. It will change people's minds about Shakespeare.   C ☐

PAPER 2 - LISTENING

You will hear someone talking on the radio about taxis and private hire vehicles in London. For each question, fill in the missing information in the numbered space.

LONDON TAXIS AND PRIVATE HIRE VEHICLES

Taxi Services
- Taxi & private hire 24 hours a day, 365 days a year.
- Pay in (14) .... *cash* ...., or with credit & debit cards.
- Not all black.
- Stopped in the (15) .... *street* .... or at cab ranks.
- Can be booked in advance.

Taxi Costs
- *Depends on time of day, distance travelled and time taken.*

Tariff 1: Monday - Friday 6 a.m. - 8 p.m.

Tariff 2: Monday - Friday 8 p.m. - 10 p.m., (16) .... *Saturday* .... & .... *Sunday* .... 6 a.m. - 10 p.m.

Tariff 3: Every night 10 p.m. - 6 a.m. & on (17) .... *public holidays* ....

Tests to become a Taxi Driver
- Criminal record check.
- (18) .... *(full) medical* .... examination.
- Knowledge of London's streets

Private Hire Vehicles
- Limousine
- Chauffer services, often known as (19) .... *minicabs* ....
- Journeys always booked in advance by visiting office or by phone.

Look at the six sentences for this part. You will hear a conversation between a man, Ben, and a woman, Lucy, about football. Decide if each sentence is correct or incorrect. If it is correct, put a tick (✓) in the box under **A for YES**. If it is not correct, put a tick (✓) in the box under **B for NO**.

	A YES	B NO
20. Ben and Lucy both enjoy watching and playing football.		✓
21. Lucy thinks Ben is the best player.	✓	
22. Ben does not like all of the training session.	✓	
23. Lucy's favourite team is Manchester United.		✓
24. Ben believes that football grounds are safe.	✓	
25. In the end they decide to go to a match together.		✓

Test 4

PAPER 1 READING & WRITING

PART 1 Questions 1-5

Look at the text in each question. What does it say? Mark the letter next to the correct explanation **A**, **B** or **C**.

Example:

0

NO BALL GAMES ALLOWED ON THE GRASS

A. You may not sit on the grass.
B. Be careful not to damage the grass while playing ball games on it.
C. All ball games are forbidden on the grass.

Example answer: | **0** | C |

1

NOTICE
All passengers are reminded that you are not allowed to eat, drink or smoke in the underground system.

 B

A. You can only smoke, eat and drink in special areas on the train.
B. You cannot drink, eat or smoke anywhere on the underground system.
C. You cannot carry packets of cigarettes on the underground system.

2

Postcard
Dear Jane,
It's beautiful here in Spain, the sun's shining and we've been to the beach almost every day! The hotel's not great, but we're out most of the time! Wish you were here,
Love Anne

 A

A. Anne does not think the hotel is very good.
B. The weather is not very good in Spain.
C. Jane wishes Anne was there with her.

3

E-mail
TO: Nick
FROM: Peter

I've found a great site that's got views of all the latest Hollywood films! Check out the articles and let me know if you want us to go to see anything.

 C

A. Nick is an actor.
B. Peter has written an article on films and wants Nick's opinion.
C. Peter wants Nick to read film reviews from an Internet site.

4

Message
David, as soon as you get this message ring dad on his mobile. Mum's broken down on the motorway and he's got to collect her.
Sam

 B

Sam wants David to
A. pick up their mother.
B. ring their dad so he will pick up their mother.
C. drive to the motorway with their dad's mobile phone.

5

Note
The boss has called an emergency meeting. Bring your marketing plan to his office tomorrow at 4.00; don't forget to tell the other staff.

 C

A. You must meet your competitors.
B. The boss does not like your marketing plan.
C. There is a problem and you must give a plan to the boss.

PAPER 1 – READING

These people (6-10) all want to see a film at the cinema. Look at the eight reviews (A-H). Decide which film would be the most suitable for each person. For questions 6-10, choose the correct letter (A-H).

6. Ian's favourite movies are horror films, but not if they contain too much blood. He would like to see something to do with mystery and ghosts.

| 6 | C |

7. Jenny wants to go with her boyfriend on a date, and wants to see something that is romantic and ideal for young people, but she knows he does not like musicals.

| 7 | E |

8. Nick has had a stressful day and wants to see a film that will help him relax and escape. He would like something funny but does not enjoy unbelievable films.

| 8 | B |

9. George is married to Sylvia and they want to see an entertaining film. They have seen many typical Hollywood movies but now they want something more light and cultural with singing or dancing.

| 9 | A |

10. Rob is interested in technology and the future and he wants a different setting from everyday situations. He also prefers films to have a message or an issue to think about.

| 10 | G |

Films of the week

A. East-side Story

This sequel to the original musical classic is definitely worth seeing. This time the romantic interest takes place between a middle-aged Italian man and a Russian woman in New York, with a sentimental message concerning love and age. Superb dance routines and vocal performances make this exceptional film as entertaining as a Broadway hit.

B. Chuckling all Day

The young comedian Steve Trumann gives us another hilarious performance as the office worker who suffers one humorous accident after another in the busy city he lives in. We get the impression that this could happen to anyone of us which perhaps helps us laugh in an understanding way.

C. Phantom Screams

In this tense psychological production, James Tyler has the same terrible dream, that spirits who want the house empty, murder him and his family. However, when the first events of his dream start to become reality, a series of enigmatic clues provide the only hope he has to save himself and the family.

D. The Soldier Returns

Despite this attempt at serious acting, action star Arnold Stallon reproduces a typically mindless performance as he plays an ex-commando who must fight a drug-lord. Arnold fights through the armies of opponents with guns, knives and bombs, as he bloodily beats each opponent.

E. Destiny of the Heart

Two young students leave high school for college, despite the fact that they were in love with each other, neither managed to tell the other. The film is set four years later when the two meet by chance at a train station. Will they separate again or live happily ever after?
A predictable but sweet romantic movie for teenagers.

F. Murder at the Office

This is a classic murder mystery from director Angela Christen. At the beginning of the film we see through the murderer's eyes, as he attacks and brutally kills his victim, a rich businessman. Next, we see a room with five suspects, all his employees, who were in the building at the time. Can you guess who did it?

G. The 23rd Century Man

The biggest science fiction film of the year does not disappoint as Michael Saunt plays an astronaut in the 23rd century who is travelling the stars with only robots and computers as company. Despite the great potential of scientific advancements the film contains warnings about the danger of losing our human nature to computers.

H. Henry V

Anyone looking for a piece of cultural entertainment should consider this classic Shakespeare play, complete with Hollywood special effects and star names. The hard reality of war in the middle ages is certainly brought to life by the tough actors as they march through France.

PART 3 | Questions 11-20

Look at the sentences below about a holiday company that organises boat trips on canals. Read the text to decide if each sentence is correct or incorrect. If it is correct, mark A. If it is not correct, mark B.

11. All the BCC's boats have been examined by an official organisation. **11 | A**

12. The BCC's holidays are all for one week or more. **12 | B**

13. Children are not allowed on the narrow boats. **13 | B**

14. You do not need previous knowledge to go on a BCC holiday. **14 | A**

15. Food is provided on the deck at lunchtime. **15 | B**

16. You can begin your holiday from different starting points. **16 | A**

17. You can travel by boat to England, Scotland and Wales. **17 | B**

18. The boats are provided with many appliances. **18 | A**

19. The BCC holidays are supposed to make you feel at ease. **19 | A**

20. You can receive a free brochure only if you order through the Internet. **20 | B**

The British Canal Company

Spoil yourself

With the British Canal Company (BCC), you'll get a real holiday in comfort and style aboard one of our tourist board inspected narrow boats.

Whether you're looking for a weekend break or a week or more, you'll have the choice of almost 100 boats, from 2 to 12 berth - ideal for couples, families and friends.

If this is your first time aboard a narrow boat, don't worry. No previous experience is necessary, as we will provide full tuition at the start of the holiday.

During the day you can cruise leisurely through unspoilt countryside, mooring perhaps at a charming canal-side pub for lunch. Then, after a lazy afternoon, relax on deck and watch the sun go down.

See for yourself

You can start your holiday from one of our four well-located bases to explore over 1500 miles of the superb inland waterways of England and Wales.

With beautiful wooden interiors, comfortable beds, hot and cold running water, showers, flushing toilets, and, in some cases, even microwaves and dishwashers. The list of home comforts is endless.

Our free, full colour brochure is packed with ideas to make your holiday afloat an experience you'll never forget. So remember how holidays used to be: easy, unhurried, with endless freedom and long lazy days, living life at an altogether more relaxing pace. A holiday with us will bring you all this and more.

What do I do now?

To obtain a free copy of our brochure simply complete the form below and send it in an envelope to the address on the following page. Alternatively you can phone or E-mail us.

PART 4 **Questions 21-25**

Read the text and questions below. For each question, choose the correct letter A, B, C or D.

Madonna

Ever since she burst onto the pop scene in the early eighties, Madonna has remained one of the most well known celebrities in the world. She has shown herself to be a talented singer, dancer, songwriter and actress. To have achieved this she undoubtedly has a strong belief in herself and her abilities.

It is possible she gained her strong personality through her tough childhood experiences. She went to a strict Catholic school, was one of many children, and her family was split up after her mother died from cancer. Eventually, in search of fame, she left college and went to New York with only her suitcase and a few dollars.

Hugely successful, often through controversy, Madonna has always known what the public and media want. She has gone from shocking clothes and pop songs, to setting trends and family life. She caused disagreement by playing feminist roles in films and featuring in pop videos with images of Jesus Christ.

Throughout all her years and different styles and phases, she has always been able to give the general public entertainment. Madonna has become one of the biggest stars on the planet, and has sold over 100 million records worldwide, making her one of the highest-earning entertainers of her generation.

Even now as she approaches fifty and is a mother, Madonna is likely to continue to entertain us for many more years, but what nobody can be sure of is exactly what she will do next!

21. **What is the writer's main purpose in writing this text?**
   A. to discuss Madonna's acting career, and encourage other pop stars to go into acting
   B. to show how well Madonna has achieved success throughout the years
   C. to remind people that money is not everything, and it comes and goes
   D. to claim that fashion always changes, and no one can stay famous forever

22. **As a child, Madonna was probably**
   A. happiest during her school days.
   B. lonely and without anyone to talk to.
   C. unhappy in New York.
   D. made stronger due to difficult events.

23. **What is true according to the text?**
   A. Madonna has always been careful not to offend the public.
   B. Madonna apologised to the Church after causing offence with a pop video.
   C. Madonna often upset people but achieved a great deal.
   D. Madonna disliked the controversy in her career.

24. **What does the writer say about Madonna's success?**
   A. She is one of the richest performers of her time.
   B. She has earned more money than many international businesses.
   C. Her success is mainly due to the American market.
   D. Her consistent style has allowed her to earn so much money.

25. **How would the writer probably describe Madonna's future?**
   A. "After so much success, acting will become more important than singing."
   B. "Family life will be the main factor in Madonna's everyday life, no more wild days!"
   C. "She'll keep on pleasing the public in a predictable way."
   D. "Madonna is sure to keep us guessing on her future plans."

PART 5 | Questions 26-35

Read the text below and choose the correct word for each space. For each question, choose the correct letter **A, B, C** or **D.**

Example: | **0** | A   B   C   D |

Magnets

A solid object that has the power to **(0)attract** iron and some other metals is called a magnet. It does this through its magnetic field, a region of force surrounding it. The **(26)**................................. the magnet, the more intense is the field.

Objects that are attracted to the magnet, feel a force **(27)**................................. as 'magnetism', when they are inside the magnetic field. This magnetic force can pass **(28)**................................. some materials. Even a weak magnet will attract a pin to the other side of a **(29)**................................. of paper, for example.

Magnets come in **(30)**................................. shapes. A familiar one is the curved horseshoe magnet. There are also bar magnets in the form **(31)**................................. a disc or a stubby cylinder. Every magnet has **(32)**................................. poles, called north and south, at opposite ends of it: at the two ends of a horseshoe magnet, for example, or on the two sides of a disc.

Powerful magnets can be **(33)**................................. by passing an electric current through wire coiled around a piece of iron. The **(34)**................................. is called an electromagnet. Magnets are **(35)**........................... in many household and everyday devices. They are also commonly used in industrial machinery, usually in the form of electromagnets.

0.	**A.** understand	**B. attract**	**C.** include	**D.** develop
26.	**A.** smaller	**B. stronger**	**C.** weaker	**D.** thinner
27.	**A.** mentioned	**B.** called	**C. known**	**D.** said
28.	**A. through**	**B.** away	**C.** outside	**D.** next
29.	**A.** pane	**B.** block	**C.** pile	**D. sheet**
30.	**A.** separate	**B. different**	**C.** unknown	**D.** identical
31.	**A. of**	**B.** in	**C.** out	**D.** up
32.	**A.** many	**B.** several	**C. two**	**D.** one
33.	**A.** found	**B.** had	**C.** done	**D. made**
34.	**A.** ending	**B. result**	**C.** conclusion	**D.** final
35.	**A. used**	**B.** made	**C.** lived	**D.** unseen

WRITING

PART 1 | **Questions 1-5**

Here are some sentences about work and jobs. For each question, complete the second sentence so that it means the same as the first, __using no more than three words__. Write only the missing words.

Example: (0) Shall I phone the manager for you?
Would you like **me to phone** the manager for you?

1. John will be at home on Saturday, if he doesn't have to work overtime.

   John will be at home on Saturday, ... *unless he has* .... **to work overtime.**

2. The secretary said, 'Andrew will leave early today.'

   The secretary said that Andrew .... *would leave* .... **early that day.**

3. This city has very few good jobs.

   .... *There aren't (are not)* .... **many good jobs in this city.**

4. You must not play games on your computer while at work.

   You are .... *not allowed* .... **to play games on your computer while at work.**

5. Helen started working at the office two years ago.

   Helen .... *has worked (has been working)* ...., **at the office for two years.**

PART 2 | Question 6

An English friend of yours is going to come to your hometown to study for a year.
Write an e-mail to your friend. In your e-mail you should

- Tell your friend how happy you are.
- Say something good about your town.
- Suggest what you will do in the first week.

Write **35-45** words.

PART 3 | Question 7-8

Write an answer to **ONE** of the questions (**7 or 8**) in this part. Write your answer in about **100** words. Put the question number at the top of your answer.

Question 7
This is part of a letter you have received from an English pen friend.

> That's everything about my house, I love it!
> What about your house?
> What do you like most about it?

Now write a **letter** to your pen friend, telling him/her about your house.

Question 8
- Your English teacher has asked you to write a story.
- Your story must begin with this title:

    My Favourite Person.

- Write your **story**.

PAPER 2   LISTENING

PART 1   Questions 1-7

There are seven questions in this part. For each question there are three pictures and a short recording. Choose the correct picture and put a tick (✓) in the box below it.

Example: *Where did the woman leave her hat?*

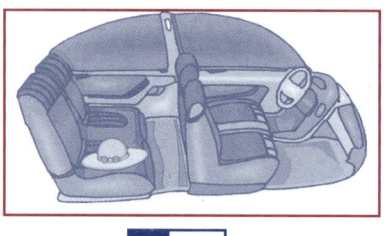

A [ ]   B [✓]   C [ ]

---

1. What time will they meet?

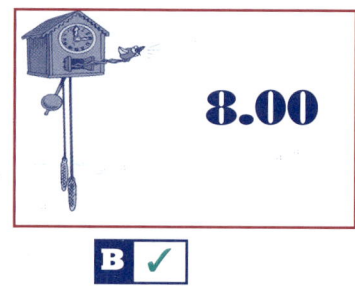

7.30   8.00   8.15

A [ ]   B [✓]   C [ ]

2. Where is the woman's diary?

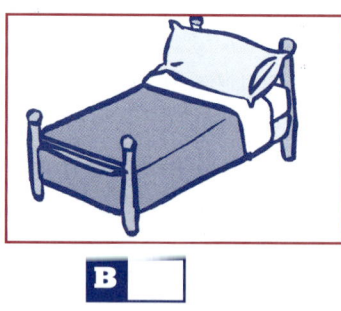
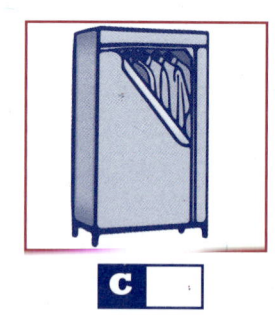

A [✓]   B [ ]   C [ ]

3. What is not open on Monday?

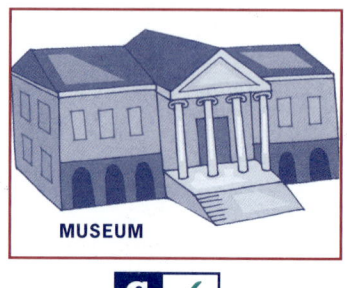

LEISURE CENTRE

MUSEUM

A [ ]   B [ ]   C [✓]

4. What will she eat?

 **A** ✓

 **B**

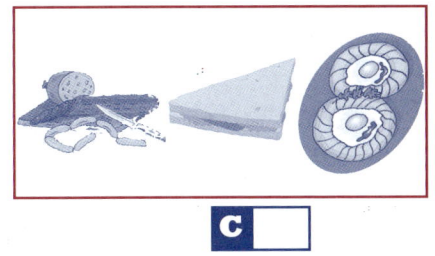 **C**

5. Where did the man go on Saturday?

 **A** ✓

 **B**

 **C**

6. What will he buy for his brother?

 **A** ✓

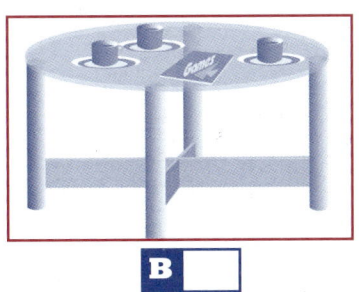 **B**

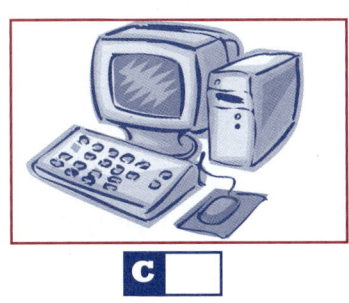 **C**

7. How will most people travel to work tomorrow?

 **A**

 **B** ✓

 **C**

PAPER 2 - LISTENING

You will hear a man, David, being interviewed about his life as a professional footballer. For each question, put a tick (✓) in the correct box.

8.   **How long has David been a professional football player?**

    A. One match.   **A** ☐

    B. Two years.   **B** ✓

    C. Four years.   **C** ☐

9.   **What is in a normal day for David?**

    A. Fitness training and tactics.   **A** ✓

    B. Fitness training and a full match.   **B** ☐

    C. Fitness training, tactics and a full match.   **C** ☐

10.   **What do the team not watch videos about?**

    A. The opposition.   **A** ☐

    B. Warming up.   **B** ✓

    C. Their own performance.   **C** ☐

11.   **What does David say about the diet of a footballer?**

    A. It is often unpleasant and bad.   **A** ☐

    B. It has lots of rice, meat and pasta.   **B** ☐

    C. Footballers have to be careful about what they eat.   **C** ✓

12.   **What is true about David's free time?**

    A. He spends most of his free time with his friends.   **A** ☐

    B. He has very little free time, except in the summer.   **B** ✓

    C. He usually does not manage to see his family.   **C** ☐

13.   **What does David say about his future ambitions?**

    A. He firstly wants to secure a regular place in the team.   **A** ✓

    B. He wants to play for a European team in the next two years.   **B** ☐

    C. He never thinks about playing in the World Cup.   **C** ☐

PART 3 | Questions 14-19

You will hear a woman talking on the radio about tours of historic houses in the south of England. For each question, fill in the missing information in the numbered space.

HISTORIC TOURS

South Elmham House

Built:	13th century by the bishops of Norwich.
Improved:	16th century by a group of **(14)** .... *(rich) Lords* ....
Features:	- Many old, valuable, wall paintings.
	- Remains of a(n) **(15)** .... *(small) (Norman) church* ..... .
Tours:	- (Including a walk), 2 p.m., £12, tea/coffee; meal bookable.

Haughley Hall

Built:	14th century (outside ruined castle).
Improved:	18th century.
Features:	- Once owned by King Henry II, currently owned by a Lord.
	- Secret **(16)** .... *hiding places* .... in the walls.
	- Two tunnels now closed.
Tours:	- 11.30 or 2 p.m., £15 with **(17)** *(traditional) lunch* .... , £12 with tea. Groups welcome.

Bedfield House

Built:	12th century by the church.
Improved:	Mid 15th century.
Features:	- Signs that protect against **(18)** .... *witchcraft* .... are on ceilings and surfaces.
	- Gardens are joined by **(19)** .... *(five) bridges* ....
Tours:	- 10.30 a.m. or 2.30 p.m., £13.50 with tea/coffee and cakes. Groups welcome.

PART 4 | Questions 20-25

Look at the six sentences for this part. You will hear a conversation between a boy, Steve, and a girl, Cathy, planning a day trip. Decide if each sentence is correct or incorrect. If it is correct, put a tick (✓) in the box under **A for YES**. If it is not correct, put a tick (✓) in the box under **B for NO**.

	A YES	B NO
20. They will go to a shopping centre outside of London.		✓
21. They will travel by coach.	✓	
22. Cathy wants to see the clothes shops mostly.	✓	
23. Steve will spend a lot of money.		✓
24. Cathy wants to go to the theatre.		✓
25. They will eat near the train station.		✓

Test 5

PAPER 1 READING & WRITING

Look at the text in each question. What does it say? Mark the letter next to the correct explanation **A, B** or **C**.

Example:

0

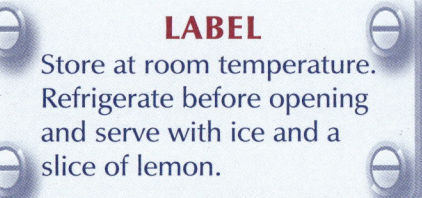

NO BALL GAMES ALLOWED ON THE GRASS

A. You may not sit on the grass.
B. Be careful not to damage the grass while playing ball games on it.
C. All ball games are forbidden on the grass.

Example answer: **0** C

1

LABEL
Store at room temperature. Refrigerate before opening and serve with ice and a slice of lemon.

A

A. Chill the drink in the fridge before you use it.
B. The drink should be served at an average temperature.
C. Keep the drink at room temperature before serving it.

2

SIGN
Private road. No public access or parking. In use 24 hours.

B

A. The car park is open to the public 24 hours.
B. It is forbidden to use, or stop on, this road.
C. Private cars are not allowed to use the road at night.

3

Notice
Thieves will be reported to the police and taken to court.

B

A. The police are watching thieves in the area.
B. The police will be informed of any stealing.
C. The court has sent the police to arrest some thieves.

4

E-mail
To: Mr. Clinton
From: Mr. Smith
Re: Museum trip.
Could you inform me how much it would cost to take my class of thirty students to the local museum? Thank you.

C

A. Mr. Smith works for the local museum.
B. Mr. Clinton wants to take a school class to the museum.
C. Mr. Smith is organising a school trip to a museum.

5

Note
Dave, Can you pick up a fresh loaf, two pies and a cream cake? Thanks, Annie

A

Where does Annie want Dave to go shopping?
A. a bakery
B. a cafeteria
C. a butcher's shop

PART 2 | Questions 6-10

*These people (6-10) are looking for a holiday destination in Greece. Look at the eight reviews (A-H). Decide which resort would be the most suitable for each person. For questions **6-10**, choose the correct letter (**A-H**).*

6. Jay wants to go to an island with lots of exciting nightlife, and also be able to visit other nearby islands for day trips.

| 6 | D |

7. Dean wants to go with a group of university students to a place where they can both enjoy nightlife and visit historic sites during the day.

| 7 | B |

8. Chris and his wife are celebrating their first wedding anniversary. They have been to some popular resorts before, but now they want to visit somewhere different and memorable.

| 8 | H |

9. Alan and his three friends want to combine days on hot beaches with their interest in outdoor activities, such as climbing and hill walking.

| 9 | E |

10. George is arranging a holiday for a group of retired couples that want to visit areas of historical importance, as well as experience the local culture. They require a relaxing and peaceful place to stay.

| 10 | G |

Recommended Greek Holiday Resorts

A. Corfu

If you want the classic Greek holiday resort, come to our new family destination in Corfu. The resort has a two-kilometre stretch of beach, which is not dominated by bars and nightclubs. Each day, however, there are special children's club activities on the main beach, some of which parents can also join in with!

B. Cape Attica

This resort is located only a few hundred metres from historic Cape Sounio, and is only a fifty minute coach trip to Athens. Daily trips to the Acropolis and other such famous landmarks in the city are available. The night bus service allows a full experience of the vibrant Athens nightlife.

C. Mount Athos

The religious peninsula known as Mount Athos is unspoilt by modern development and contains some of the most beautiful natural scenery in the whole country.
This male-only area is home to monasteries from various countries, and is peaceful enough for a saint.

D. Mykonos

Mykonos is now internationally famous for its glamorous clubs and bars, which attract many of the rich and famous from the Greek celebrity world. The unique party atmosphere of this island is not to be missed. Ferries are also available to provide day trips to many of the nearby islands.

E. Crete

The south of Crete contains some of the most exotic beaches, swept by the hot winds of Africa. After you've cooled off in the sea, the famous canyon, the longest in Europe is well worth a visit for the very active and fit. Some remarkable scenery can be discovered if you put in the legwork.

F. Thessalonica

Experience shopping in the wide streets of Greece's second city. All the top designers are to be found in the commercial centre. After this why not enjoy some traditional nightlife in one of the many live music clubs in the city.

G. Peloponnesian Tour

Enjoy a tour of the sights of the historic Peloponnesian Peninsula, taking in Sparta, Argos and Corinth. In each location you will stay in comfortable and peaceful hotels, which specialise in the best of local food and wines.

H. Santorini

For an experience that's unique among the Greek islands, the volcanic island of Santorini has a magic of its own, even though it doesn't have as many beaches as some others. The spectacular views of the sunset are not to be missed and give full justification to Santorini being a place for people who are in love.

PART 3 | Questions 11-20

Look at the sentences below about the transport museum of East Anglia. Read the text to decide if each sentence is correct or incorrect. If it is correct, mark **A**. If it is not correct, mark **B**.

11.	You have the opportunity to travel on old trams and trolleybuses.	11	A
12.	There are several other museums similar to this one in Britain.	12	B
13.	Only historical British vehicles can be seen at the museum.	13	B
14.	Informative exhibits teach you about the transport of earlier years.	14	A
15.	The museum has its own high-speed railway site.	15	B
16.	Refreshments are available after visiting the railway.	16	A
17.	The museum is equipped for parents and the disabled.	17	A
18.	Classic vehicle owners and clubs are preferred to school groups.	18	B
19.	If you arrange a birthday at the museum they will automatically book extra entertainment.	19	B
20.	The staff offer their services without payment.	20	A

Where the past passes by...

Enjoy a truly interactive historical experience, with rides on our classic trams and trolleybuses. Trace the history of public and private transport through fascinating displays of buses, cars, steamrollers, commercial vehicles, and many transport-related artefacts.

A Museum on the Move

Here at Carlton Colville you will find a museum unique to the last detail, for this is the only place in the British Isles where visitors can not only view, but also ride on all three principal forms of public transport from the earlier part of the 20th Century.

- With vehicles from home and abroad, there's something for everyone!
- Explore the Exhibition Halls housing vehicles and artefacts!
- Learn about the transport of times past through informative displays!
- See vehicles of the past in our period street with authentic street furniture!
- Visit us on a Special Event day to see our preserved bus fleet in action!

The East Suffolk Light Railway

As an added attraction our very own light railway, with its fleet of 2ft steam engines, sleepily makes its way around the site. This is a real life representation of this type of railway that was used to carry both passengers and goods and is always a firm favourite with young and old alike.

History in Motion

When all the excitement is over, relax in the Terminus Tearooms with its wide choice of drinks and snacks, or browse the museum shop where you're sure to find gifts and souvenirs for all ages and interests! To make sure everyone can join in the fun, many of the museum's buildings are wheelchair and pushchair accessible; we have an accessible tram and train, and both baby changing and disabled facilities.

An Extra Special Visit

The museum is pleased to open for pre-booked club, society or school groups from April to September. Visits from classic vehicle owners and clubs are just as welcome. Any vintage vehicle can be displayed on the museum site during normal opening hours on days other than those of specific special events. Or how about a birthday party! The museum cafe can offer a range of buffet options to suit all ages and tastes. You can really enjoy your birthday at our museum!

Contact Us

Should you wish to contact us at the museum there are a number of ways in which this can be done. As we are all volunteers we cannot promise to answer the phone or reply to a letter, fax or e-mail straight away, but we will always do our best.

PART 4 | Questions 21-25

Read the text and questions below. For each question, choose the correct letter A, B, C or D.

Axel Thorn

I have had many years as a successful rock star, but will always remember my roots and how I formed my first band. At sixteen I was still growing up in a bad part of town. I didn't have any way to express myself; I was frustrated at the terrible state of the neighbourhood and the unfairness that existed. Just a few miles away rich people lived who had everything, while we had nothing, and could only hope for the worst of jobs.

One night, while I was at a friend's house we found a pair of electric guitars, and started playing. We pretty much taught ourselves the music, and when a couple of other guys joined, who really knew how to play, I knew we had something. With my lyrics, I could express far more emotion and communicate with other people.

Soon after that we set up our own band. The songs we write are still very important to us. They're about voicing how we feel about the problems and issues around us, crime, unemployment, exploitation, and the inequality present in the country.

Of course, we are also expressing our own dreams and desires. It can be sensational to be on stage and have twenty thousand people sing the songs that you write, songs that are about people like them, and in the end, they are for people like them.

Our music has been very popular and is worth listening to, as it is the ordinary people who have made it such a success. We sing what we feel, so we're sure that if people listen to the music, they'll understand the message too.

21. **What is Axel Thorn's main purpose in writing this text?**
    A. to explain the music industry to poor people
    B. to describe how and why he took up music
    C. to explain why he has been so successful
    D. to describe the life of a rock star

22. **What could a reader learn about Axel's childhood?**
    A. His family always treated him terribly.
    B. He was surrounded by rich people.
    C. He grew up in a poor area of town.
    D. His family had the worst jobs in the area.

23. **How does Axel describe his lyrics?**
    A. They express his feelings on serious issues.
    B. They are written by a professional songwriter.
    C. They are about the problem of international conflict.
    D. They are the most important thing in his life.

24. **What does Axel say about performing on stage?**
    A. It was his great dream, as he always loved attention.
    B. They only perform in front of crowds of twenty thousand or more.
    C. Most people at the concerts do not understand his music.
    D. He feels amazing when the crowd sing his own songs.

25. **How might Axel describe being in a band?**
    A. Being in a band is the greatest thing I could ever hope to do. The best part is the money and being famous.
    B. We are now a hugely successful band all over the world. I want to make more pop and commercial music to make more money.
    C. Music was always important to me as a way to comment on social problems and communicate with the people.
    D. The enjoyment I got when I was younger is no longer there, I don't feel so connected with the people as I used to.

PAPER 1 – READING

PART 5 Questions 26-35

Read the text below and choose the correct word for each space. For each question, choose the correct letter **A, B, C** or **D**.

Example:

0	A	B	C	D
			▄▄	

Our Homes: Now and Then

(0) _Everyone_ needs a home where they feel sheltered and safe. Today we live **(26)**.................................... modern flats and houses, **(27)**.................................... have air-conditioning to keep us cool, and heating to keep us **(28)**.................................... . There is electricity for lighting and supplies of gas or oil for the heating. Hot and cold water **(29)**.................................... from the taps and dirty water disappears **(30)**.................................... the drains. Many of our homes have balconies or gardens.

In the past, people made their homes from **(31)**.................................... that they found nearby. When we look at different houses we can tell how old they are from the materials used and the way they were built.

It was different long **(32)**.................................... , people did not have water in their homes **(33)**.................................... there were no electric lights. To keep warm they sometimes made .... inside their homes. With a fire started they **(35)**.................................... also cook their food and heat water.

0.	**A.** Everything	**B.** Anything	**C. Everyone**	**D.** Anyone
26.	**A.** on	**B.** for	**C.** in	**D.** with
27.	**A.** who	**B.** which	**C.** where	**D.** whose
28.	**A.** hot	**B.** light	**C.** warm	**D.** safe
29.	**A.** flows	**B.** finds	**C.** flies	**D.** floats
30.	**A.** up	**B.** towards	**C.** on	**D.** down
31.	**A.** places	**B.** materials	**C.** parts	**D.** money
32.	**A.** back	**B.** then	**C.** ago	**D.** time
33.	**A.** and	**B.** because	**C.** if	**D.** until
34.	**A.** flames	**B.** food	**C.** fires	**D.** furnaces
35.	**A.** should	**B.** could	**C.** must	**D.** will

WRITING

PART 1 | Questions 1-5

Here are some sentences about food and drink. For each question, complete the second sentence so that it means the same as the first, **using no more than three words**. Write only the missing words.

Example: *(0)* The town has many exotic restaurants.
In the town **there are** many exotic restaurants.

---

1. I have never met such a clever man as the chef.

   The chef is the .....*cleverest / most clever*..... **man I've ever met.**

2. We could not sit down at the restaurant, as there were so many people.

   There were .....*too many*..... **people at the restaurant for us to sit down.**

3. Only a small group of French monks make this wine.

   This wine .....*is only made*..... **by a small group of French monks.**

4. 'Did you buy Italian food?', Jim asked Carol.

   Jim asked Carol if she .....*had bought*..... **Italian food.**

5. My parents thought that we should eat healthier food.

   My parents wanted .....*us to eat*..... **healthier food.**

PAPER 1 - WRITING

PART 2 | Question 6

An English friend of yours wants to know what school is like in your country.
Write an e-mail to your friend. In your e-mail you should

- Tell him how big your school is.
- Say something about your friends.
- Explain what subjects you like best.

Write **35-45** words.

PART 3 | Question 7-8

Write an answer to **ONE** of the questions (**7 or 8**) in this part. Write your answer in about **100** words. Put the question number at the top of your answer.

Question 7

This is part of a letter you receive from an English pen friend.

> I had a great time that summer. Have you ever had a great summer holiday? Tell me all about what you did.

Now write a **letter** to your pen friend, answering his/her questions.

Question 8

- Your English teacher has asked you to write a story.
- Your story must begin with this sentence:

  I couldn't believe what my dad had just said.

- Write your **story**.

PAPER 2   LISTENING

PART 1   Questions 1-7

There are seven questions in this part. For each question there are three pictures and a short recording. Choose the correct picture and put a tick (✓) in the box below it.

Example: *Where did the woman leave her hat?*

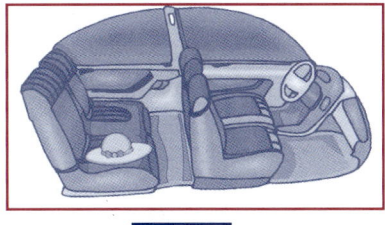

A ☐   **B** ✓   **C** ☐

1. What did the boy's uncle buy him for Christmas?

A ☐   **B** ✓   **C** ☐

2. What job does Michelle's father do?

A ✓   **B** ☐   **C** ☐

3. How will Steve get to school tomorrow?

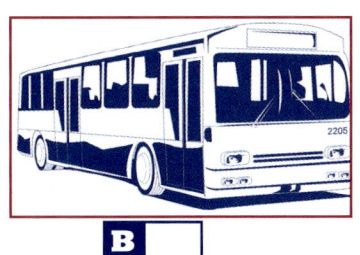

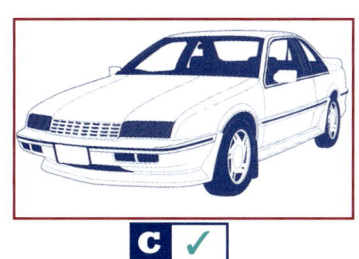

A ☐   **B** ☐   **C** ✓

4. What will the weather be like on Saturday?

 **A** ✓

 **B**

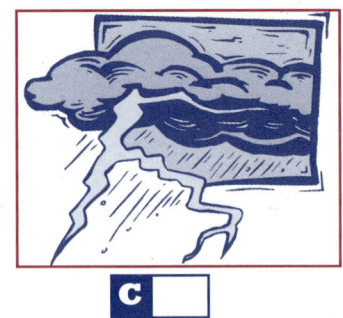 **C**

5. Who robbed the bank?

 **A** ✓

 **B**

 **C**

6. What will the woman do last?

 **A**

 **B**

 **C** ✓

7. What does the man want to do at the weekend?

 **A**

 **B** ✓

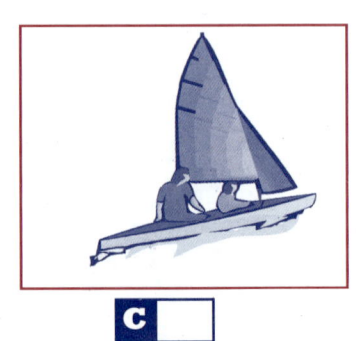 **C**

PART 2 | Questions 8-13

You will hear someone talking about a race he entered with his wife. For each question, put a tick (✓) in the correct box.

8. What does the man say about the good and bad days on the journey?

A. There were more bad days than good ones.

B. There were not many bad days.

C. There were only a few good days.

A	
B	✓
C	

9. What is said about the cost of taking part in the race?

A. It cost them £30,000 each.

B. It cost a lot of money, time and effort.

C. The man's work supported the couple financially.

A	
B	✓
C	

10. What is true about the race?

A. There were two people in each boat.

B. There were 7 boats in the race.

C. The boat was 12 metres long.

A	✓
B	
C	

11. What is true about the teams in the race?

A. There were six all-female teams.

B. No other husband and wife team entered.

C. Two teams were only made up of women.

A	
B	
C	✓

12. What was true of Hannah Snell?

A. She was a ship's captain in the 1700's.

B. She fought as a Marine.

C. She was killed in battle.

A	
B	✓
C	

13. What does the man say about the start of the race?

A. He wanted to beat the other families.

B. The weather conditions seemed excellent.

C. The teams were friendly with each other.

A	
B	
C	✓

PAPER 2 - LISTENING

You will hear an announcement at a fitness centre. For each question, fill in the missing information in the numbered space.

HEALTH WEEK

Course Guarantees:

1. Become healthier.

2. Learn new **(14)** ....*exercise*........................ techniques.

3. Work hard.

Things to Take:

- A good pair of trainers.
- A(n) **(15)** ....*tracksuit*.................... .
- Shorts and T-shirts.
- Swimming costume for the pool.

Programme

First Day:
- Weighing
- Health questionnaire.
- Plan with **(16)** ....*(specific) targets*............ for each person.

Weekdays: Morning: exercise sessions in the gym.
                        personal trainer to check you exercise correctly.
              Afternoon: healthy snack.
                        exercises in the pool.
              (17) ....*relaxation*............ in the spa.

Last Day: Individual weighing, assessment and progress check.
              Discussion on **(18)** ....*fitness strategies*............ & maintaining progress in everyday life.

Price:
- 25% discount
- Total cost **(19)** ....*105 pounds / £105*............ for one week.

Look at the six sentences for this part. You will hear a conversation between a man, Barry, and his daughter, Elizabeth. Decide if each sentence is correct or incorrect. If it is correct, put a tick (✓) in the box under **A for YES**. If it is not correct, put a tick (✓) in the box under **B for NO**.

	A YES	B NO
20. They have lived in their new house for four months.		✓
21. Elizabeth's favourite activity is going to the cinema.		✓
22. Barry was worried about crime in London.	✓	
23. Elizabeth wants to be an actor when she grows up.	✓	
24. Barry thinks Elizabeth is not focused on her exams.		✓
25. Elizabeth is captain of the volleyball team.		✓

Test 6

PAPER 1 READING & WRITING

PART 1 Questions 1-5

Look at the text in each question. What does it say? Mark the letter next to the correct explanation **A**, **B** or **C**.

Example:

0

NO BALL GAMES ALLOWED ON THE GRASS

A. You may not sit on the grass.
B. Be careful not to damage the grass while playing ball games on it.
C. All ball games are forbidden on the grass.

Example answer: 0 C

1

To: Brian
From: Sue
Are you still feeling down?
You should come out with us to cheer yourself up. I'll come and collect you Saturday at six if you like.

B

Why has Sue emailed Brian?
A. To see if he is sick.
B. To invite him to do something.
C. To tell him that she is feeling depressed.

2

Due to circumstances beyond our control, the shop will close at 4 p.m. instead of 5 p.m. on Wednesday. We apologise to our customers for any inconvenience this may cause.

B

A. The shop usually closes early once a week.
B. An unavoidable problem has affected the shop.
C. The shop will be closed all afternoon on Wednesday.

3

20% deposit reserves any item in the shop

A

A. Pay part of the price and we will keep any item for you.
B. 20% reduction off any item in the shop if you pay now.
C. No items can be bought without paying a deposit first.

4

FREE ADMISSION TO GALLERY AFTER 6.30 PM.

B

A. You must enter the gallery by 6.30 pm.
B. There is no entrance fee to the gallery after 6.30 pm.
C. You are not allowed to enter the gallery less than half an hour before it closes.

5

Hey John,
We've decided to go to Berlin for the weekend. Do you want to come and enjoy some good food with us? We need you to translate!
Tina

C

A. Tina wants John to help with the cooking.
B. Tina speaks German well.
C. Tina needs John's language skills.

PART 2 **Questions 6-10**

These people (6-10) all want to borrow a book from the library. Look at the eight reviews (A-H). Decide which book would be the most suitable for each person. For questions **6-10**, choose the correct letter (**A-H**).

 6. Brian is twenty-two and has just graduated with a degree in history. He enjoys reading about real people who have done something unusual or exciting in their life.  **6** C

 7. Marie is a primary school teacher. She enjoys reading books that transport her to another world or a completely different life from her own. She also likes romantic novels.  **7** B

 8. Bob is a retired scientist. He enjoys doing quizzes and solving puzzles because he has a very analytical mind.  **8** G

 9. Angie doesn't have a lot of time to read so she enjoys books that she can read a little bit at a time. She particularly likes books about people and human relationships.  **9** A

 10. John likes detective stories. He doesn't like anything that is too complicated because he doesn't want to have to concentrate too much while he is reading.  **10** D

BOOK REVIEWS

A. Journeys with my family
This book of short stories isn't actually about travelling at all, even though the title may suggest otherwise. It is a collection of studies of how people interact with their families. Often funny and also often heartbreaking, these short stories show both the best and the worst of people.

B. The enchanted April
An ad for a castle to rent on the Italian Riviera brings together four very different women. Their beautiful environment helps them make discoveries about themselves, life and love. A novel that you won't want to put down once you start reading it.

C. Living with the bushmen
This is the true account of Richard Berk's search for the African bushmen and their amazing acceptance of his presence in their timeless world. Berk managed, against all odds, to live with the bushmen for six months, learning their language and exploring their ancient culture. A remarkable story about a remarkable anthropologist.

D. Trouble in the suburbs
A light-hearted crime story about a private investigator on his final case before retirement. However, the investigation takes an unexpected turn of events and the hero is put in some dangerous situations. A good read for those who don't want to be challenged too much.

E. The King of all KINGS
This story of an imaginary Egyptian pharaoh has some interesting archaeological facts and some beautifully drawn maps and diagrams. But unless you have a passion for Ancient Egypt, it probably wouldn't be a gripping read.

F. The History of advertising
A surprisingly interesting look at how the media has affected and reflected our lifestyles. This non-fiction book examines how advertising has developed over the years and how we now accept images that would have been censored in the past.

G. The Connection
Not an easy-reading book. This complex novel takes the reader into a world of intrigue and overlapping events that all have an effect on each other. There is, however, one common factor that links everything together. Can you work out what that common factor is before all is revealed in the final chapter?

H. The Lost Leopard
The story of a snow leopard, orphaned by hunters, which trekked across miles of frozen land searching for a home. This book is sponsored by the Leopard Sanctuary and its message about the corrupt fur trade is clear and powerful.

PART 3   Questions 11-20

Look at the sentences below about a holiday in Asia. Read the text to decide if each sentence is correct or incorrect.
If it is correct, mark A. If it is not correct, mark B.

11. This trip is for people who like to travel in luxury.   **11** **B**

12. You will get lots of exercise on a cyclo.   **12** **B**

13. This would make a good family holiday.   **13** **B**

14. Evening meals are not included in the price.   **14** **A**

15. You will be shown around by knowledgeable people.   **15** **A**

16. You will have a room all to yourself.   **16** **B**

17. You will stay in the White Palace.   **17** **B**

18. You will have lunch with a farmer in My Tho.   **18** **B**

19. You will probably see food you've never seen before.   **19** **A**

20. You will travel on some man-made rivers.   **20** **A**

"Images of Asia"

The main focus of this holiday is to introduce you to Vietnam and Thailand on our specially designed tour. Sightseeing will be by traditional "cyclo" (3-wheeler bicycle rickshaws: The passenger sits in front of the driver). There will also be excursions by local train, hydrofoil and boat. The holiday concentrates on the south of the two countries. Look out for buildings combining French colonial and Chinese styles; for ornate temples, for bicycle traffic jams; for traditional arts such as the unique "water puppet" performances; and, of course, for the reminders of the infamous long-running war, such as the former Presidential Palace.

We regret children are not accepted on this tour.

THE PRICE INCLUDES

- Scheduled flights.
- 12 nights accommodation inc 5 nights in Bangkok.
- In Vietnam, 7 breakfasts and 2 lunches.
- Excursions and visits as described.
- Experienced local guides.
- UK dept tax of £20.
- Prices per person sharing twin.

Not included: Vietnam visa. Local departure taxes. Optional insurance. Booking conditions apply.

EXCURSION ONE
Vung Tau/Saigon

Morning sightseeing tour of Vung Tau, visiting the White Palace, Lighthouse, statue of St Jacques and a "cyclo" ride around the centre. Return to Saigon's city quay by hydrofoil up the Saigon River from the South China Sea. 2 nights at the Garden Plaza.

EXCURSION TWO
Mekong Delta

Drive into the heartland of the Mekong River Delta, through rice fields, orchards and market gardens. On reaching the town of My Tho, board small boats for a leisurely ride along the river. Land at an offshore 'garden island' for a guided walk and visit a typical farmer's home. See beekeeping and the growing of many unusual vegetables, herbs and fruits. Board a sampan, sliding along small, artificial canals to Thoi San Island for lunch. Visit Vinh Trang pagoda before returning to Saigon, through Cholon, the city's China Town.

PART 4 Questions 21-25

Read the text and questions below. For each question, choose the correct letter **A, B, C** or **D**.

ALICE BRADLEY

I guess you could say that acting is in my blood as my mother and father are both actors, my grandfather was a theatre musician and my grandmother was a singer and dancer. I suppose it seemed normal for me to do a little turn for family and friends. I certainly wasn't a shy wallflower.

I went to drama school in London on Saturdays from the age of six. We were taught how to sing and dance as well as act so I was a good all-rounder by my teens.

Once I'd left school I went to drama school in London full-time to do a degree. I must admit that I had a slight lapse in commitment at that time, for a period of about six months. I joined up with the party crowd and danced the nights away and slept late most mornings. It was only when my personal tutor told me that I was on my final warning that I realised I might be expelled.

After the shock of that realisation I got my act together very quickly and ended up graduating with a first.

The Royal Shakespeare Company gave me my first real role and I acted alongside some great names in the world of the stage. Now of course I'm better known for my Hollywood roles and people will probably be amazed to hear that I first walked the boards as a Shakespearean actor.

21. **What is the writer's main purpose in writing the text?**
  A. to express her ambitions for the future
  B. to discuss plays by Shakespeare
  C. to talk about her acting career
  D. to describe how she lives

22. **What does the writer say about her childhood?**
  A. Her parents forced her to be an actor.
  B. She was surrounded by entertainers.
  C. She was reluctant to perform for her family.
  D. She was too young to enjoy drama school when her parents first sent her.

23. **What happened when the writer was a full-time drama student?**
  A. She was nearly told to leave the course.
  B. She had an argument with her personal tutor.
  C. She concentrated on developing as a serious dancer.
  D. She worked as a dancer in the evenings.

24. **What does the writer say about working as a Shakespearean actor?**
  A. She found it boring after a while.
  B. It is what she is mostly known for.
  C. It was something she had to do to get into Hollywood.
  D. It gave her the chance to work with distinguished actors.

25. **Which of the following is the best description of the writer?**
  A. The young actor who is developing a career.
  B. The actor who has followed in her parents' footsteps and made the leap from Shakespeare to Hollywood.
  C. The reluctant actor who struggled through drama school and became a Hollywood director.
  D. The rebel actor whose wild life is affecting her career but who is now trying to mend her ways.

Read the text below and choose the correct word for each space. For each question, choose the correct letter **A, B, C** or **D**.

Example:

		A	B	C	D
0				▬	

Look after your eyes

The eye is one of the **(0)** _most_ astonishing organs in the body, working constantly to turn light into streams of nerve impulses **(26)**............................... the brain can convert into visual images. But **(27)**............................... our vision dominates how we understand the world around us, most people take it **(28)**............................... granted, giving little thought to the complex processes that **(29)**............................... them to see, **(30)**............................... one day they realise they have a problem. From midlife onwards **(31)**............................... different eye conditions become common and **(32)**............................... the age of 45 most people have noticed that they can't see as well as they once **(33)**............................... . **(34)**............................... of these problems can be cor-rected with glasses or contact lenses, while **(35)**............................... need surgery.

0.	**A.** very	**B.** too	**C. most**	**D.** so
26.	**A.** who	**B. which**	**C.** whom	**D.** whose
27.	**A. although**	**B.** however	**C.** whatever	**D.** despite
28.	**A.** with	**B.** at	**C. for**	**D.** on
29.	**A.** grant	**B.** endure	**C. enable**	**D.** provide
30.	**A.** besides	**B.** moreover	**C.** furthermore	**D. until**
31.	**A. several**	**B.** few	**C.** maximum	**D.** most
32.	**A. by**	**B.** to	**C.** on	**D.** with
33.	**A.** should	**B. could**	**C.** ought	**D.** will
34.	**A.** Few	**B.** Others	**C. Some**	**D.** All
35.	**A.** those	**B.** these	**C.** additional	**D. others**

WRITING

PART 1 — Questions 1-5

Here are some sentences about travelling. For each question, complete the second sentence so that it means the same as the first, <u>using no more than three words</u>. Write only the missing words.

Example: *(0) I like travelling by ship more than by plane.*
I __prefer to__ travel by ship than by plane.

1. Why don't you go on a cruise?

   If I were you, ... I would go .... **on a cruise.**

2. It's too expensive to stay in that hotel.

   It isn't .... cheap enough .... **to stay in that hotel.**

3. If you don't remember your passport, you won't be able to go on the plane.

   You won't be able to go on the plane unless .... you remember .... **your passport.**

4. You missed the plane because you checked in too late.

   If you hadn't checked in so late, you .... would not have .... **missed the plane.**

5. There aren't many tourists in this area.

   There are very .... few tourists .... **in this area.**

PART 2 | Question 6

An English friend of yours called Tom sent you a CD for your birthday, which you liked very much.
Write a card to Tom. In your card, you should

- Thank him for the CD.
- Say which song you liked best.
- Suggest another singer that Tom might like.

Write **35-45** words.

PART 3 | Question 7-8

Write an answer to **ONE** of the questions (**7 or 8**) in this part. Write your answer in about **100** words. Put the question number at the top of your answer.

Question 7

This is part of a letter you receive from an English pen friend.

> What do you do at the weekend generally?
> Where do you like to spend time with your friends?

Now write a **letter** answering your pen friend's questions.

Question 8

- Your English teacher has asked you to write a story.
- Your story must begin with this sentence:

    I couldn't believe my eyes.

- Write your **story**.

PAPER 2 LISTENING

PART 1 | Questions 1-7

There are seven questions in this part. For each question there are three pictures and a short recording. Choose the correct picture and put a tick (✓) in the box below it.

Example: *Where did the woman leave her hat?*

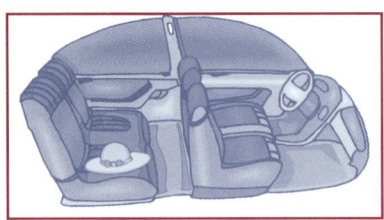

A

B ✓

C

---

1. What has the woman received for her birthday?

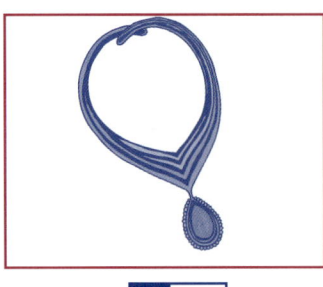

A

B

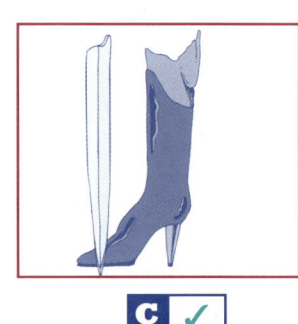
C ✓

2. What did the man forget to buy?

A

B ✓

C

3. What is the date of the party?

A ✓

B

CALENDAR

27

C

4. What's the weather like now?

A ✓   **B**   **C**

5. What form of transport is unaffected?

  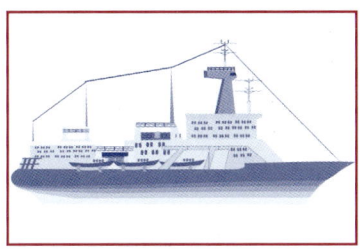

A   **B** ✓   **C**

6. What is Julie studying?

A   **B** ✓   **C**

7. Where is Billy now?

A   **B**   **C** ✓

PAPER 2 - LISTENING

PART 2 Questions 8-13

You will hear someone reviewing some local arts and entertainment events. For each question, put a tick (✓) in the correct box.

8. The art exhibition

A. is boring.

B. is shocking.

C. has a mixture of amateur and professional artists.

A	
B	✓
C	

9. "Raisin in the Sun" is

A. a comedy.

B. about religion.

C. about life decisions.

A	
B	
C	✓

10. What is said about the film?

A. The whole family may enjoy it.

B. Parents will be bored.

C. It would only appeal to Americans.

A	✓
B	
C	

11. What is special about Friday night at the "Med Food Restaurant"?

A. The chefs are related.

B. The food will be free.

C. Customers can have a free drink.

A	
B	
C	✓

12. The government is trying to

A. encourage people to be healthier.

B. force children to do sport.

C. stop children from being too competitive.

A	✓
B	
C	

13. The speaker suggests that

A. Supermarkets don't sell healthy food.

B. The market is fun for all the family.

C. The market is good for a night out.

A	
B	✓
C	

PART 3   Questions 14-19

You will hear a holiday rep welcoming a new group of guests to a hotel. For each question, fill in the missing information in the numbered space.

The Oasis Hotel

You can find Steven in his office between 10 and 11 a.m. or (14) ....6............... and ....7................... p.m.

Everything is included in the excursion price except (15) ....*(a packed) lunch*............ .

Children under the age of (16) ....*twelve / 12*................ are not allowed to go on the excursion.

The creche and toddler group closes at (17) ....*11.30*................... in the morning.

It costs (18) ....*£5*............ an hour for an aerobics class.

On Sunday you can attend a (19) ....*water aerobics*............ class in the pool at 10 o'clock.

PART 4   Questions 20-25

Look at the six sentences for this part. You will hear a conversation between a man, John, and a woman, Anna, about their jobs. Decide if each sentence is correct or incorrect. If it is correct, put a tick (✔) in the box under **A for YES**. If it is not correct, put a tick (✔) in the box under **B for NO**.

		A YES	B NO
20.	Anna has to drive throughout the night from meeting to meeting.		✔
21.	Anna generally has a problem getting to sleep.		✔
22.	John had been expecting his promotion.		✔
23.	John is nervous about doing the accounts.	✔	
24.	John denies he is looking for a girlfriend.	✔	
25.	Anna will probably go to the Cactus Club.	✔	

Test 7

PAPER 1 READING & WRITING

PART 1 Questions 1-5

Look at the text in each question. What does it say? Mark the letter next to the correct explanation **A, B** or **C.**

Example:

0

> **NO BALL GAMES ALLOWED ON THE GRASS**

A. You may not sit on the grass.
B. Be careful not to damage the grass while playing ball games on it.
C. All ball games are forbidden on the grass.

Example answer: **0** C

1

> Use by end of April 2013. Consume within three days of opening or freeze immediately after opening.

C

A. You must eat the contents as soon as the container is opened.
B. The container must not be opened while frozen.
C. The contents must be thrown away after April 2013.

2

> The staff meeting arranged for 4 o'clock on Thursday will be held a day earlier at the same time. Please let me know by 5 o'clock today if you can't attend.

 B

A. The meeting will be held at 5 o'clock today.
B. The meeting will be held at 4 o'clock on Wednesday.
C. The meeting will be held at 5 o'clock.

3

> No entry beyond this point without a security pass. Passes can be obtained at reception. Proof of identity is required.

 C

A. The receptionist will give everyone a security pass.
B. Under no circumstances can anyone go beyond this point.
C. People without a pass will not be allowed past this point.

4

> **MESSAGE**
> Gerry, I've gone to the shops to get some herbs for the chicken. Can you peel the carrots and keep an eye on the potatoes so they don't burn in the oven?

 A

A. The potatoes are already roasting.
B. The chicken is already cooked.
C. The carrots are being cooked now.

5

> **Children must not enter the bar unless accompanied by an adult.**

 B

A. Under no circumstances are children allowed in the bar.
B. Children are allowed in the bar if they are with someone aged 18 or over.
C. Children may enter the bar with the permission of an adult.

PART 2 | Questions 6-10

These people (6-10) all want to watch something on TV tonight. Look at the eight TV programmes or films (A-H). Decide which programme would be the most suitable for each person. For questions 6-10, choose the correct letter (A-H).

 6. Barbara is a history teacher but she's also very interested in art. She is interested in programmes about real life, people or events. She prefers non-fiction to fiction and is fascinated by other cultures. **6** | C

 **7.** Adam doesn't have a lot of time to watch TV as he is always in a hurry. He enjoys quizzes and gameshows because he's a very competitive person. **7** | E

 **8.** Barry is an interior designer. He has lived in several European countries and often travels to gain ideas for his house designs and decoration. **8** | F

 **9.** Mark is a seventeen-year-old student. He plays in a rock band and enjoys action films with lots of adventure. He also enjoys films about people that he can relate to in some way. **9** | A

10. Sarah enjoys thrillers and horror films. She likes to try to solve mysteries and gets bored if there isn't much action. She prefers fiction to non-fiction. **10** | D

WHAT'S ON TV TONIGHT?

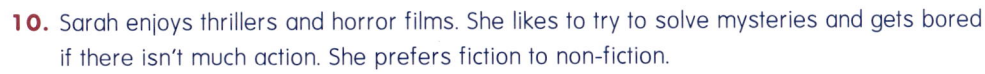

A. Drumline *(Charles Stone III, 2002) 6pm, Sky Movies 1*
A tough kid from the wrong side of the tracks joins a snooty school where his rhythmic prowess is put to the test in the military marching band. But he's survived so long on street-smarts alone, will he be able to reveal a soft side under that bullish exterior and will this loner learn to work in a team? Well it's no worse than any other teen movie. The drumming scenes are impressive climaxing with a tense drum-off with the rival team. As a drumming movie it's hard to beat!

B. Journey of Life *9pm, BBC1*
Steve Leonard leads this new five-part exploration of how we got here, from single-celled organisms to blue whales. As you'd expect there's lots of great footage: today - flying fish, sharks and coral. As well as a brutally simple demonstration of the survival of the fittest theory with some baby turtles on a beach, there's a graphic demonstration of one of nature's more unpleasant defence mechanisms: a sea cucumber that literally throws its guts up when attacked.

C. Horizon *9pm BBC2*
Documentary examining the rise and fall of the Moche people who vanished without trace, despite ruling the northern coast of Peru, constructing imposing pyramids and founding an empire which lasted for hundreds of years. The programme reveals artefacts and other evidence recently uncovered by scientists and archaeologists, which have finally allowed them to piece together what really happened to one of the greatest civilizations of the ancient world.

D. Murder One *9pm, FX*
A welcome repeat for this cult Steven Bochco crime show from 1996. A bit like a slower 24, it follows a single murder case, with each episode showing a single day. Daniel Benzali holds everything together as Teddy Hoffman, LA's top criminal attorney, hired to defend shady millionaire Tichard Cross (Stanley Tucci) when his mistress's 15-year-old sister is found dead. Packed with lots of actors you'll recognise - this is meaty stuff, with Hollywood players, political wrangling and dodgy deals.

E. Masterchef Goes Large *6.30pm BBC2*
A revamp for the old format, with contestants having to create a new recipe from scratch in 30 minutes, before the three most promising are sent to the kitchens of London's La Porchetta, where they must prepare simple Italian meals as quickly as possible. Their final challenge is to make a two-course meal for judges John Torode and Gregg Wallace who will decide which of them will go through to Friday's quarter-final.

F. A Dream Home Abroad *8pm Five*
George Clarke follows the efforts of a wealthy north London couple to transform a 200-year-old farmhouse in Piedmont, Italy, into the house of their dreams. Despite having no money worries and providing a realistic deadline for the completion of the project, work commitments mean they cannot be away from the UK for long stretches, requiring them to trust the builders to complete the job largely unsupervised.

G. Faith *9pm BBC1*
William Ivory's story of love, deceit and betrayal is set against the backdrop of the Miners' Strike of 1984-1985. The year-long conflict forces two sisters and their husbands to reassess their relationships with each other as they struggle to make ends meet, setting the scene for a showdown that is both political and personal and will change their lives for ever.

H. Dispatches *9pm Channel 4*
An investigation into the working lives of traffic wardens, with hidden cameras revealing the extent of the abuse they are faced with on a day-to-day basis from angry and often violent motorists. The programme also exposes the strategies and tactics that wardens employ to ensure suitable punishments are handed out to those who have violated parking laws.

PAPER 1 - READING

PART 3 Questions 11-20

*Look at the sentences below about Berlin. Read the text to decide if each sentence is correct or incorrect. If it is correct, mark **A**. If it is not correct, mark **B**.*

11. The Hamburger Bahnhof Museum contains modern art.

11	A

12. You can catch a train from the Bahnhof Museum.

12	B

13. The museum is impressive by day and night.

13	A

14. KaDeWe is the biggest shopping centre in the world.

14	B

15. You don't have to be rich to shop at KaDeWe.

15	A

16. The Mitte area is a cultural area.

16	A

17. Young people would probably avoid the Kreukberg neighbourhood.

17	B

18. KaDeWe is the best place to buy a second-hand book.

18	B

19. You will be bored in the Turkish coffee shops if you don't take a book with you.

19	B

20. Berlin has plenty of nightlife in the Mitte area.

20	A

"Exploring Berlin"

With its fascinating history and its currently in-vogue urban scene, Berlin really is a city of contrasts, and after all those scenic strolls it's time for some art. Berlin's "museum for the present" Hamburger Bahnhof has a variety of work from contemporary European artists as well as a large collection of works by Andy Warhol. Housed in an impressive 18th-century railway terminal, the museum is a sleek, clever refit of a classical building. If you think it's impressive by day, be sure to stroll by at night when it's bathed in a striking blue light.

For fantastic shopping, KaDeWe is Europe's largest shopping centre. It's also suitably glam with a Reichstag style glass dome and an entire top floor devoted to gourmet foods, including over 100 varieties of wurst-sausage heaven! From Dior to Diesel, KaDeWe has a good mix of the affordable and the sky high.

But if shopping centres leave you cold, the Mitte area might be more your scene. The new face of the former east, this area hosts the highest density of clubs in the city and is packed with art galleries, cool shops and bars. The Kreukberg neighbourhood is especially well-known for alternative culture blending a hip, too-cool-for-school scene with a cosmopolitan vibe. Head to the Turkish coffee shops for some serious people watching and don't forget to take a classic European novel with you - there are plenty of great second-hand bookstores around if you left yours at home. Whoever wants to seriously go out in Berlin, also does so in Mitte in relaxed and loungy clubs like "Delicious Donutes" or "Mr Wonka's".

PART 4 | Questions 21-25

*Read the text and questions below. For each question, mark the letter next to the correct answer **A, B, C** or **D**.*

JEFF STRINGER - JUDGE

I've always enjoyed being with other people and I suppose I've always had a strong opinion about what is wrong and what is right, even from when I was a young child. That used to irritate my brothers and sisters because I would grass on them if they did something wrong. They had secrets that they wouldn't share with me and I probably missed out on a lot, because of that. Not that I blame them.

I actually studied history at university and then, in my final year, I had a work placement in a lawyer's office. I was fascinated from day one and as soon as I graduated I applied to do a degree in law. I get a real buzz from fighting for justice, no matter what kind of case it is. It can be hard not to get emotionally involved at times. You just have to follow your head and not your heart in such situations.

I make it a personal rule not to take my work home with me. Once I leave the court, I switch off and concentrate on my family. They will always be my number one priority.

21. Which of the following best describes the writer?
  A. A strict family man.
  B. A workaholic who puts work before family.
  C. A man who cares about his family and his clients.
  D. A judge that everyone fears.

22. Why did the writer's brothers and sisters get annoyed with him?
  A. Because he was always misbehaving.
  B. Because he was their parents' favourite child.
  C. Because he followed them all the time.
  D. Because he got them into trouble.

23. What does he say about his job?
  A. He has a lot of job satisfaction.
  B. He often gets emotionally involved with his clients.
  C. He always wins a case.
  D. It doesn't affect him emotionally.

24. What does the writer do at the end of the working day?
  A. Finish off any work that he has at home.
  B. Leave all his work problems at the court.
  C. Tell his family all about his working day.
  D. Worry overly about his family.

25. Which of the following is the best description of how the writer feels about life?
  A. positive and satisfied
  B. tense and worried
  C. ambitious but stressed
  D. relaxed but bored

Read the text below and choose the correct word for each space. For each question, choose the correct letter **A, B, C or D.**

Example answer:

0	A	B	C	D
			▬	

We all need a good night's sleep

According (**0**) _to_ the Sleep Council, 20 million people in the UK aren't (**26**) .... enough sleep - and some experts now believe that "sleep debt" can impair your metabolism and disrupt hormone levels. To (**27**) .... out how (**28**) .... you need, says sleep expert Professor Chris Idzikowski, director of the Sleep Assessment and Advisory Service, (**29**) .... your alarm for when you (**30**) .... to get up, then count back six to eight hours, (**31**) .... on how much shut-eye you feel you need. Try to go to bed at this time every night, and get up at the same time - even at weekends. If you (**32**) .... feel tired during the day, go to bed earlier by 15 minutes a week until you wake up refreshed. So if you (**33**) .... go to bed at 11pm, say, go at 10.45pm for a week. If you're still tired, try going at 10.30 the (**34**) .... week, and so on. Remember, too: a weekend afternoon nap can help (**35**) .... up for any missed hours in the week.

0.	**A.** for	**B.** with	**C. to**	**D.** at
26.	**A.** making	**B.** doing	**C.** being	**D.** getting
27.	**A.** work	**B.** put	**C.** let	**D.** take
28.	**A.** many	**B.** much	**C.** some	**D.** lots
29.	**A.** place	**B.** set	**C.** make	**D.** locate
30.	**A.** need	**B.** must	**C.** should	**D.** would
31.	**A.** counting	**B.** relying	**C.** needing	**D.** depending
32.	**A.** yet	**B.** but	**C.** never	**D.** still
33.	**A.** gradually	**B.** remarkably	**C.** normally	**D.** definitely
34.	**A.** previous	**B.** last	**C.** following	**D.** formerly
35.	**A.** do	**B.** make	**C.** keep	**D.** put

WRITING

PART 1 **Questions 1-5**

Here are some sentences about leisure and sport. For each question, complete the second sentence so that it means the same as the first, **using no more than three words**. Write only the missing words.

Example: *I'm better at basketball than Mark.*
        Mark isn't **as good at** *basketball as I am.*

1. The reporter described the game in detail.

   The reporter gave a ...*full/ detailed   description/account   of*... **the game.**

2. You can borrow my racket, but you must be careful with it.

   You can borrow my racket as ...*long as you*... **are careful with it.**

3. She left early because she did not want to miss the start of the match.

   She left early ...*so that she*... **would not miss the start of the match.**

4. "I'm sorry but I don't want to play tennis", said Harry.

   Harry said that he ...*did not want*... **to play tennis.**

5. All the players did their best apart from Alan.

   Alan was the only player ...*who did not*... **try his best.**

PAPER 1 - WRITING

PART 2   Question 6

An English friend of yours, called Sarah, gave a dinner party last night, which you enjoyed. Write a card to Sarah. In your card, you should

- Thank her for dinner.
- Say how much you enjoyed the food.
- Invite her to dinner.

Write **35-45** words.

PART 3   Question 7-8

Write an answer to **ONE** of the questions (**7 or 8**) in this part. Write your answer in about **100** words. Put the question number at the top of your answer.

Question 7

This is part of a letter you receive from an English pen friend.

> In your next letter, please tell me about traditional food in your country. What's your favourite meal? Do you eat fast food?

Now write a **letter** answering your pen friend's questions.

Question 8

- Your English teacher has asked you to write a story.
- Your story must begin with this sentence:

    Jackie didn't know whether to laugh or cry.

- Write your **story**.

PAPER 2   LISTENING

PART 1   Questions 1-7

There are seven questions in this part. For each question there are three pictures and a short recording. Choose the correct picture and put a tick (✓) in the box below it.

Example: *Where did the woman leave her hat?*

A

B ✓

C

---

1. What is the woman talking about?

A

B

C ✓

2. What is the man's job?

A

B ✓

C

3. Where are they?

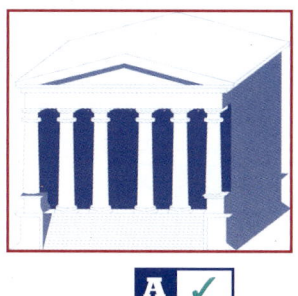

A ✓

B

C

4. What is the woman going to do on Sunday?

A ✓

B

C

5. What are the people talking about?

A

B ✓

C

6. Where do the people work?

A

B ✓

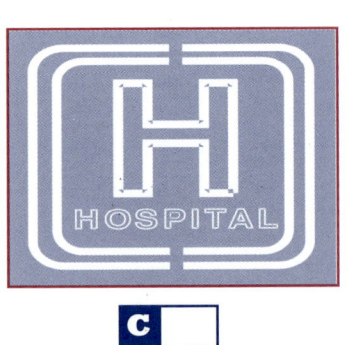

C

7. What is dangerous about the weather tonight?

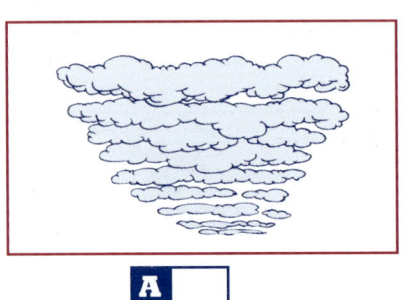

A

B

C ✓

PART 2 | Questions 8-13

You will hear a man talking about a new community centre that is about to open. For each question, put a tick (✓) in the correct box.

8. What is the man's main aim in this report?

A. to raise finances for the centre

    A ☐

B. to ask people to help run the centre

    B ☐

C. to encourage different generations to use the centre

    C ✓

9. What is said about the building?

A. It is brand new.

    A ☐

B. It's a historic building that's been changed.

    B ✓

C. It needs a lot of work done on it.

    C ☐

10. Who will Sally be able to help?

A. People recovering from a leg operation.

    A ✓

B. People trying to improve as athletes.

    B ☐

C. People who want to avoid getting injured.

    C ☐

11. What is <u>not</u> provided regularly for older people?

A. dancing

    A ☐

B. lectures

    B ✓

C. Bingo

    C ☐

12. Who can John help?

A. only teenagers

    A ☐

B. mostly pensioners

    B ☐

C. people of all ages

    C ✓

13. What is said about the playgroup?

A. Mums are expected to supervise their children.

    A ☐

B. Mums can go to work and leave their children there all morning.

    B ✓

C. Mums will be paid if they want to help out with the playgroup.

    C ☐

You will hear a woman talking about an art holiday. For each question, fill in the missing information in the numbered space.

Spanish Art Holidays

Daily Programme

8 - 9	Breakfast on the patio.
	(14) .... *self-service* .... buffet-style breakfast.
9.30	Leave hotel and walk to painting location.
10 - 10.30	**(15)** .... *Demonstration* .... of painting by teacher, using watercolour
	or acrylic paint or drawing with pencil or **(16)** .... *charcoal* ....
10.30 - 12.30	Guided art lesson in landscape painting.
12.30 - 13.30	**(17)** .... *Picnic* .... lunch. All food and drinks provided by hotel.
	Collect packed lunch after breakfast from **(18)** .... *reception* ....
13.30 - 15.30	Art lesson continues.
15.30 - 16.30	Group **(19)** .... *tutorial* .... to discuss the day's work.
17.00	Arrive back at hotel.
18.30	Evening meal in the restaurant.

Look at the six sentences for this part. You will hear a conversation between a man and a woman, about travelling.
Decide if each sentence is correct or incorrect. If it is correct, put a tick (✓) in the box under **A for YES.**
If it is not correct, put a tick (✓) in the box under **B for NO.**

		A YES	B NO
20.	Amanda likes to travel with other people.	✓	
21.	George always feels a bit nervous in Europe.		✓
22.	Amanda always takes lots of photographs when she's on holiday.		✓
23.	George sometimes misses having company when he's travelling.	✓	
24.	George writes when he's travelling.	✓	
25.	George initially travelled a lot because he had to.	✓	

Test 8

PAPER 1 READING & WRITING

PART 1 Questions 1-5

Look at the text in each question. What does it say? Mark the letter next to the correct explanation **A, B** or **C**.

Example:

0

> **NO BALL GAMES ALLOWED ON THE GRASS**

A. You may not sit on the grass.
B. Be careful not to damage the grass while playing ball games on it.
C. All ball games are forbidden on the grass.

Example answer: | **0** | C |

1

> **Memo**
> All staff should submit their reports by Wed for the Fri meeting.

| **B** |

A. All reports must be handed in at Friday's meeting.
B. All reports are needed before Friday's meeting.
C. Staff will present their reports at Friday's meeting.

2

> Jane,
> George phoned to say that he needs his camera back before Saturday for Bob's wedding. Can you drop it at his place because he is too busy to collect it? He wants to know if you've been invited to the wedding because he can give you a lift.
> Sue

| **C** |

A. George is inviting Jane to a wedding.
B. George wants to borrow Jane's camera.
C. George is making both a request and an offer.

3

> **If red light flashes, check copier for paper jam. If there is no jam, turn off copier and restart it. If toner is low red light will flash on and off.**

| **A** |

A. If paper is stuck in the copier, the red light will come on.
B. If the red light flashes, you must turn off the copier.
C. If the red light flashes replace the toner and paper.

4

> **Please do not block the driveway. Access required at all times for loading and deliveries.**

| **C** |

A. Parking is only allowed at restricted times.
B. Deliveries must not be left here.
C. No parking here at any time.

5

> **Gift Voucher**
> Dear member,
> Introduce a friend to the gym and receive a free health and beauty session including massage.
> Valid till 31st December.

| **A** |

A. This is an offer for people who already belong to the gym.
B. This is a special package for people joining the gym before the end of the year.
C. If you and a friend join the gym now, you will get a free massage.

PAPER 1 - READING

These people (6-10) are looking for a holiday. Look at the descriptions of eight holidays (A-H). Decide which holiday (A - H) would be most suitable for each person (6 - 10). For questions 6-10, choose the correct letter (A-H).

6. Jackie is 18 and wants to go on holiday with her best friend Sarah. They are both starting university in September to study archaeology. They want to relax and swim a lot but also want to go on some excursions. They don't have much money.

 **6 | E**

7. John is retired. He loves birdwatching. He and his wife would like to go somewhere beautiful and peaceful. They don't want to have to cook on holiday and they would prefer to stay in a place that is not noisy in the evenings.

 **7 | B**

8. Stephen is very sporty and easily gets bored. He doesn't enjoy sitting on the beach all day. He likes meeting new people on holiday and enjoys lively, late nights out. He'd prefer accommodation without meals included.

 **8 | D**

9. Sandra and Dave have two young children aged six and eight. They like to go to places where there are facilities for children and adults. Dave quite enjoys watersports but Sandra prefers to play on the beach with the children.

 **9 | A**

10. Mary is 68. She is a widow. She likes to visit interesting places and is very interested in history, art and culture. She doesn't want to cook on holiday and likes to meet new people. She enjoys being in warm countries.

 **10 | H**

Holiday Choices

A Oceanview Village
Our beautiful holiday village offers self-catering accommodation in beautiful surroundings close to the beach. There is evening entertainment every night and an afternoon kids' club which is run by our team of trained staff. Excursions are available three times a week.

B Oaktree Park Hotel
Situated in beautiful grounds in the countryside, Oaktree Park offers first-class accommodation with a delicious menu offered by our award-winning chef. The landscaped grounds include a stunning lake and nature reserve. A beautiful retreat for anyone who wants to get away from it all for a while.

C Kidsland Adventure Park
A child's heaven, *Kidsland* caters for children aged 11 to 18. Accommodation is in ten-bed chalets with adult supervision. We offer sport, art and craft, computer technology, music, cookery lessons and lots more. Leave your children with us for a week or two and they will make friends for life. All meals included and entertainment provided every night.

D Bob's Diving Centre
We offer courses for both beginners and more advanced divers. Also on offer are various watersport activities including jetskis, surfing and water volleyball. Self-catering accommodation at affordable prices with a handy shop on-site for all your supplies. Evening entertainment arranged every night plus a weekly barbecue.

E Sandybeach Hotel
Situated in a small but lively resort. Sandybeach hotel is only a two-minute walk from a glorious beach. There are plenty of bars and restaurants nearby and a nightclub where you can dance until the early hours of the morning. Breakfast and evening meal are included in the remarkably cheap price and best of all, two day trips to local places of interest and historical sights are included in the package, too.

F Desert Walking Holidays
Give yourself a challenge this year and cross a desert. Organised trips (camels included to carry your bags). Professional guides will lead you through the sand. Campfire cooking and fantastic landscapes. Trek all day and enjoy quiet nights round the campfire under starry skies.

G Scandinavian Cruises
Experience the beauty of the north. Watch the amazing Northern Lights in the Scandinavian sky. Double or single cabins available with full-board catering. Don't forget to bring your winter coat for those romantic moonlit walks on deck in the snow!

H Woodside House
A beautiful hotel in the heart of the city but surrounded by lovely gardens. Come and enjoy a relaxing holiday in luxury. Within easy walking distance of the main sights and places of culture. We also offer art classes and lectures on cultural issues. Learn to make a ceramic pot or improve your painting or photography skills. Sorry, no children allowed.

PART 3 | Questions 11-20

*Look at the sentences below about the city of Rome. Read the text to decide if each sentence is correct or incorrect. If it is correct, mark **A**. If it is not correct, mark **B**.*

11. The historic centre of Rome is easily accessible on foot.　　| 11 | A |

12. Only local residents may drive in the centre of Rome.　　| 12 | B |

13. The buses in Rome are efficient but very slow.　　| 13 | B |

14. Romans like to own their own business.　　| 14 | A |

15. Most Italian tax is spent on the city of Rome.　　| 15 | B |

16. The train service in Rome has been greatly improved.　　| 16 | A |

17. Italians tend to live a long life.　　| 17 | A |

18. The number of foreign residents in Rome has decreased lately.　　| 18 | B |

19. It is possible that the Italian population could disappear one day.　　| 19 | A |

20. Family bonds are still very strong in Italy.　　| 20 | A |

"ROME"

Getting around in Rome

Although Rome is a vast city, most of the major sights are within walking distance of the historic centre, defined by the twisting Tiber river to the west, the sprawling Villa Borghese park to the north, the Roman Forum to the south and the central train station, Stazione Termini, to the east. Vatican city and the charming Trastevere are on the west bank of the Tiber.

Environment

Traffic and air pollution are Rome's greatest environmental hazards. Efforts to reduce traffic have increased dramatically in recent years: special permits are needed to drive in the city centre, strict regulations govern levels of gas emissions from motor vehicles and scooters, public transport is slowly being upgraded and a network of electric buses has been introduced. Despite these measures, many city monuments - and the health and enjoyment of visitors - is still at risk from pollution.

Economy

Tourism generates 12% of Rome's economy with the rest largely coming from banking, fashion, insurance, printing and publishing. The city council itself is one of the biggest employers while many Romans working in the private sector are self-employed, an aim of the majority of the population.

The mainstays of the city's budget are the annual 'garbage tax' (a form of municipal tax) paid by residents and its share of taxes paid to the national government. Rome receives a fairly low share of the tax pool compared to other cities; just 150 euro per person while Naples and Milan receive 524 euro and 232 euro respectively.

Rail and telecommunications services were recently boosted with some 1 billion euro being spent on both upgrading the rail network and laying fibre-optic cables throughout the city.

Society and culture

Rome's ageing population reflects the demographic trend throughout Italy, the only country in the world where the old outnumber the young, thanks to a combination of low birth rates and longevity. The population is increasing, however, thanks to the influx of immigrants. Official records suggest almost a quarter of a million (8% of the city's population) are foreigners, although the number is likely to be considerably higher if you take illegal immigrants into account.

Some 85% of Italians are Catholic with the remainder made up of Muslims, Protestants and Jews. Despite the falling birth rates - which demographers warn could lead to the extinction of the Italian race in 200 years if not reversed! - the family is of utmost importance in Roman and Italian society. The majority stay in the family home until well into their 30s, a situation made worse by high unemployment and house prices. Even then, very few men (and not many more women) move more than a few kilometres from Mum's cooking and washing machine!

PART 4 **Questions 21-25**

Read the text and questions below. For each question, mark the letter next to the correct answer A, B, C or D.

Getting fit and slim

You started the year in fine form, made a promise to yourself to get fit and slim, joined a gym and started a diet. But what happened to those gym visits and the lettuce diet? At least half of us who try to get fit and thinner give up after less than a month. Many people blame their failure on lack of time. Lack of willpower was highly important too.

 Much of this is down to the way we set unrealistic fitness goals - a flat stomach in eight weeks and a celebrity diet plan - instead of trying the boringly practical long-term fix of exercising a bit more and eating a bit less. Most fitness clubs get an influx of new members from January to March, but their use of the gym tends to decline after that. So how do you beat the temptation to give up? First, don't expect to fail as soon as you start - be positive, even if you've failed before. Many people are fooled into believing that they need to follow an expensive eating plan. This is simply not true. The answer is to soul-search for the thing that really interests and motivates you. It's fine to have small motivations, but you should write them down and put them together to make a list of things to keep you going.

You also need to change the way you think about things. Women feel particularly guilty about doing the three-hour-a-week exercise routine, thinking it 'selfish time' that takes them away from responsibilities to family and friends. It is better to regard this as vital 'self-care' time. People also think three hours is a lot of time out of their week, but we spend around 98 hours a week awake - and the other 95 we are just sitting around.

21. Where might this text be found?
- **A.** In a novel.
- **B.** In a diary.
- **C.** In a newspaper.
- **D.** In a proposal.

22. How would you describe this text?
- **A.** entertaining
- **B.** sarcastic
- **C.** informative
- **D.** aggressive

23. People tend to give up a fitness regime because
- **A.** they have achieved their goals.
- **B.** they expect too much of themselves.
- **C.** they become too tired.
- **D.** they can't afford to continue.

24. In order to continue a successful fitness programme
- **A.** you need to find a strong and lasting reason.
- **B.** you need a soul-mate to exercise with.
- **C.** you can't avoid suffering.
- **D.** your friends and family will have to suffer.

25. Which headline would best suit the text?
- **A.** Exercise - it's not worth the effort.
- **B.** Don't overtire yourself.
- **C.** Going to the gym is a waste of time.
- **D.** You can get fit if you really want to.

PART 5   Questions 26-35

Read the text below and choose the correct word for each space. For each question, choose the correct letter **A, B, C** or **D**.

Example answer:

0	A	B	C	D
			■	

Tomatoes - the whole truth

Leading scientists have **(0)** *announced* that tomatoes can be of great benefit **(26)**................................ our health. A lot of research has been **(27)** .... out in recent years. It's the whole tomato **(28)** .... may lower cancer risks, not individual compounds, **(29)** .... to new research. Experts have discovered that taking the antioxidant lycopene - **(30)** .... is found in tomatoes, but is increasingly popular **(31)** .... a health food supplement because of its link to a reduced risk of cancer - did not work as **(32)** .... as eating whole tomatoes. Scientists believe people **(33)** .... eat them in pastas, salads, tomato juice and pizza. Recent findings suggest that the risks **(34)** .... poor eating habits cannot be reversed with a pill. We shouldn't **(35)** .... easy solutions to a complex problem.

0.	A. called	B. shouted	C. *announced*	D. told
26.	A. in	B. with	C. to	D. at
27.	A. carried	B. taken	C. made	D. looked
28.	A. who	B. where	C. whom	D. that
29.	A. depending	B. suggesting	C. discussing	D. according
30.	A. which	B. what	C. when	D. while
31.	A. to	B. as	C. on	D. to
32.	A. good	B. better	C. well	D. more
33.	A. would	B. should	C. must	D. did
34.	A. of	B. to	C. on	D. for
35.	A. experience	B. direct	C. expect	D. inspect

WRITING

PART 1 Questions 1-5

Here are some sentences about smoking. For each question, complete the second sentence so that it means the same as the first, <u>using no more than three words.</u> Write only the missing words.

> **Example:** Smoking on buses is not allowed.
> You are not **allowed to smoke** on buses.

---

1. Fewer people smoke than they used to.

   Not .... *as many* .... **people smoke as they used to.**

2. I tried to stop smoking but it was very difficult to do.

   Although I tried to stop smoking, I .... *could not give* .... **up easily.**

3. We left the bar because it was too smoky.

   It was .... *so smoky* .... **that we left the bar.**

4. George suggested asking the doctor to help me stop smoking.

   George said, 'Why don't you .... *ask the doctor* .... **to help you stop smoking?'**

5. I don't have the strength to stop smoking.

   I'm not .... *strong enough* .... **to stop smoking.**

PART 2 | Question 6

You have just been to a new restaurant for the first time and you think your friend Paul would like it.

Write an email to Paul. In your email you should:
- explain where the restaurant is
- tell him what you ate
- say why you think he'd like it

Write **35-45** words.

PART 3 | Question 7-8

Write an answer to **ONE** of the questions (**7 or 8**) in this part. Write your answer in about **100** words. Put the question number at the top of your answer.

Question 7
This is part of a letter you receive from a pen friend in another country.

> So, I have decided that it's time for me to visit your country. Where would you recommend I go? What is the weather like in August? Can I find cheap accommodation? Write and tell me what you think.

Now write a **letter** answering your pen friend's questions.

Write your letter in about 100 words.

Question 8
Your English teacher has asked you to write a story.

Your story must have this title:

One of the most important days of my life.

Write your **story** in about 100 words.

PAPER 2   LISTENING

PART 1   Questions 1-7

There are seven questions in this part. For each question there are three pictures and a short recording. Choose the correct picture and put a tick (✓) in the box below it.

Example: *Where did the woman leave her hat?*

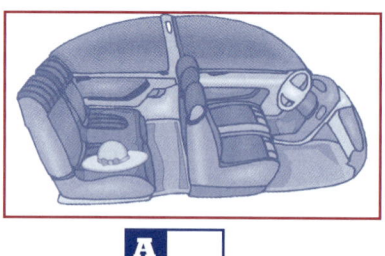

A ☐

B ✓

C ☐

1. What will they have for dinner?

A ☐

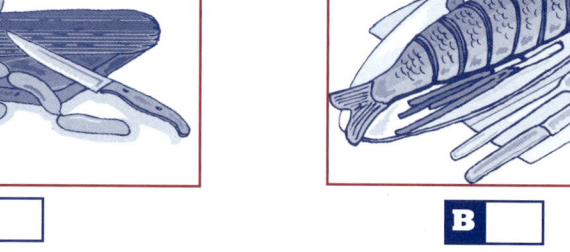

B ☐

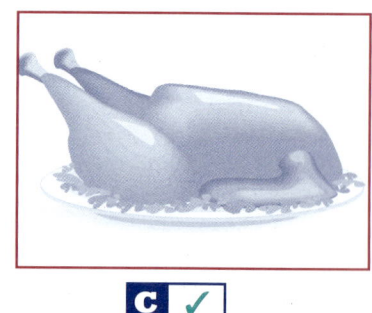

C ✓

2. What's the time?

A ✓

B ☐

C ☐

3. Which dress does Jenny buy?

A ☐

B ☐

C ✓

4. Where will the man go first after work?

A ☐

B ✓

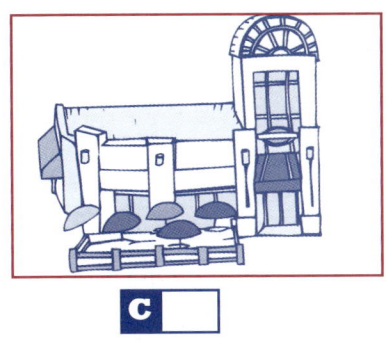

C ☐

5. How did the woman break her arm?

A ☐

B ✓

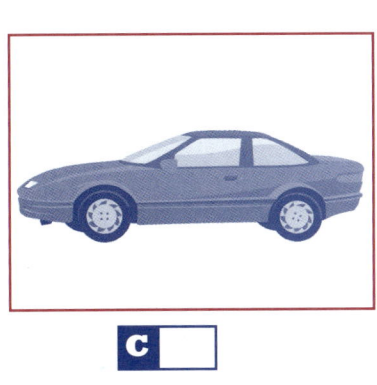

C ☐

6. Where is the remote control?

A ☐

B ☐

C ✓

7. Where did they stay on holiday this year?

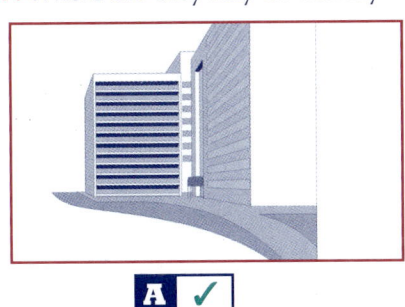

A ✓

B ☐

C ☐

PART 2 Questions 8-13

You will hear an interview with a woman who suffers from panic attacks, where she suddenly gets frightened for no reason. For each question, put a tick (✓) in the correct box.

8. **What caused Margaret's first panic attack?**

   A. She was overstressed at work.

   B. She was very tired.

   C. Nobody knows.

A	
B	
C	✓

9. **What does Margaret say about panic attacks?**

   A. They are worse than a heart attack.

   B. They are as frightening as a heart attack.

   C. You usually only ever have one in your life.

A	
B	✓
C	

10. **How did Margaret feel about her first panic attack?**

   A. angry

   B. shocked

   C. frustrated

A	
B	✓
C	

11. **Why did Margaret's husband buy her a camera?**

   A. to keep her mind off her fear

   B. to give her a new career

   C. because she'd always wanted one

A	✓
B	
C	

12. **Why did Margaret forget where she was at the lake?**

   A. She had a panic attack.

   B. She became confused.

   C. She was concentrating on the bird.

A	
B	
C	✓

13. **Why is it important that Margaret leaves her camera at home soon?**

   A. It will show that she is better.

   B. She has become addicted to photography.

   C. Her husband thinks she is being unsociable.

A	✓
B	
C	

PART 3 | Questions 14-19

You will hear a radio announcement about a competition. For each question, fill in the missing information in the numbered space.

Win a 'dream night' at the theatre

There are **(14)** ......_four_...... pairs of tickets to be won.

Performance times:

Mid week   7.30 p.m.

Tuesday-Thursday afternoons **(15)** ...._2.30 p.m._....

Saturday afternoons   2 p.m.

Ticket prices: From £11 - **(16)** ...._£24.50_....

Tickets for children available at **(17)** _half price_....

To book:

Telephone or book **(18)** ...._online_....

Competition **(19)** ...._closes / finishes_.... June 13th.

PART 4 | Questions 20-25

Look at the six sentences for this part. You will hear a conversation between a girl, Alison, and a boy, Bob, about pets. Decide if each sentence is correct or incorrect. If it is correct, put a tick (✔) in the box under **A for YES**. If it is not correct, put a tick (✔) in the box under **B for NO**.

		A YES	B NO
20.	Bob thinks a dog would be good company for Alison's grandma.	✔	
21.	Bob doesn't like dogs.		✔
22.	Bob has found homes for the kittens.		✔
23.	Alison would be happy to work at the dogs' home without getting paid.	✔	
24.	Bob thinks Alison is mad.		✔
25.	Bob and Alison will go to the dogs' home together.		✔

Test 9

PAPER 1 READING & WRITING

PART 1 Questions 1-5

Look at the text in each question. What does it say? Mark the letter next to the correct explanation **A**, **B** or **C**.

Example:

0

> **NO BALL GAMES ALLOWED
> ON THE GRASS**

A. You cannot sit on the grass.

B. Be careful not to damage the grass while playing ball games on it.

C. All ball games are forbidden on the grass.

Example answer: **0** | C

1

> **Caution!
> Floor slippery
> when wet!**

 A

A. You should be careful.

B. You may not walk on the floor.

C. It is raining.

2

> **Message**
> Hi Toby,
> Is your sister driving you to band practice today? If so, could I get a lift? Otherwise I'll have to ride the bus - mum's working.
> Thanks,
> Holly

 B

Holly is asking

A. if there is band practice.

B. about travel arrangements.

C. for advice.

3

> **E-mail**
> **To:** Lynn   **From:** Kate
>
> What are you doing this afternoon? Do you want to go to the cinema? Call me if you're free.

 A

A. Kate wants to see a movie.

B. They have changed their plans.

C. There is an offer at the cinema.

4

> Contains no sugar, artificial flavours, or preservatives.

 C

It would be seen on

A. a menu.

B. a piece of luggage.

C. a food package.

5

> Hi Mike,
> Don't forget to pick up a pint of milk at the super-market on your way home from school!
> Thanks

 B

A. Mike must take milk to school.

B. Mike needs to buy milk.

C. Someone forgot something.

PART 2 | Questions 6-10

These students (6-10) want to do some sort of after-school activity. Below there are some different classes (A-H). Offered at a Community Centre. Decide which activity (letters A-H) would be the most suitable for each person (numbers 6-10). Write the correct letter for each number.

6. **Ian** loves computers and video games. He also writes a journal every day, which he likes to read to his friends because his stories make them laugh. One of his teachers said he should start a blog, but he doesn't know what that is.

| 6 | F |

7. **Laura** wants to study web design and page layout software. She loves the Japanese culture and Japanese comics and dreams of being an exchange student there one day.

| 7 | C |

8. **Alison** is quiet and shy. She does not like fighting but she gets teased and bullied at school, and wishes she was better at standing up for herself.

| 8 | A |

9. **Beth** is training to be a violinist. She practises many hours every day and is very serious about her music studies. Her parents are worried that she is spending too much time sitting indoors and say she should go out more often with her friends. She likes sports but has not tried any so far.

| 9 | H |

10. **James** wants to be a doctor. He loves music and sports, but his main priority at the moment is his chemistry and maths exams. If he doesn't pass the class he will never be able to get a scholarship to go to medical school.

| 10 | E |

AFTER-SCHOOL CLASSES & ACTIVITIES

A. Martial Arts
We will use techniques from several different martial arts disciplines to help you build your physical strength, but more importantly your mental strength and self-confidence. Learn how to avoid conflict through confidence in your own ability to defend yourself.

B. Drawing for Comics
Do you love making drawings to entertain your friends? If so, why not develop your talent? We will help you nurture your own personal style and give you tips on the comics industry. Who knows, you could be the creator of the next *Micky Mouse* or *Calvin and Hobbs*!

C. Conversational Japanese
Learn to speak Japanese from a native speaker, while also learning about the culture and customs of this unique country. We will focus on practical language use, and use real materials like magazines and videos as learning tools.

D. Travel Writing
Wish you were born in the time of the great explorers? Is there nothing you love more than an adventure? Do you enjoy telling the tale afterwards? Well, there's still a place for the travelogue in today's world. You will read some of the great travel writing of the past, and develop your own storytelling talents using your everyday experiences; whether it's a trip to visit relatives in the next town, or the morning walk to school.

E. Maths Drop-In Tutorial
Need extra help with your Maths lessons? We offer a friendly, free drop-in service to meet your individual needs. Our tutors will help you get motivated and keep motivated. And if you need a break there are refreshments and a board game corner.

F. Website Design and Construction
Are you a budding photographer who spends hours reading others' photography blogs, or a computer geek with a dream of entertaining an audience? Well, we will give you the skills you need to build your own "stage" and find your audience. All you need to bring is some computer skills and a desire to put yourself out there to be heard or seen.

G. Jazz and Improvisation
Come and take your music practice to a new level, and have fun at the same time. We will focus on the creative aspects of music through the exploration of jazz and jamming together as a group.
(For more advanced music students; audition required).

H. Football Team
Join us for a fun way to keep fit, get out of the house, and meet new friends! Football is a fast-paced, exciting sport where team work is critical. No football or even sports experience necessary; we will teach you all the skills you need.

PART 3 Questions 11-20

Look at the statements below about the history of computer games. Read the text below to decide if each statement is correct or incorrect. If it is correct, mark A. If it is incorrect, mark B.

11. The first video games were used to make defence systems.   **11** B

12. Most homes contained a mainframe computer in the 70s.   **12** B

13. Students developed mainframe games to earn money.   **13** B

14. The first arcade games were black and white.   **14** A

15. Pac-Man is an arcade game.   **15** A

16. Arcade games were most popular in the late 70s.   **16** B

17. Arcade games became less popular as consoles improved.   **17** A

18. Modern game equipment is getting smaller.   **18** A

19. Online games are always played alone.   **19** B

20. You can try out an old-fashioned arcade game at George's Games.   **20** A

The History of Computer Games
brought to you by George's Games

Early Ideas
The origin of video games lies in early missile defence systems in the late 1940s. These were later adapted into simple games during the 1950s. Eventually video games diverged into different types: mainframe, arcade, console, personal computer and later handheld games.

Mainframe Games
Game development blossomed in the early 70s, using huge University mainframe computers. There is little record of these games, as they were not marketed, or available to the public. The students creating them often did so illicitly by making questionable use of very expensive computing resources, and so kept their work secret.

Rise of the Video Arcade
The arcade game industry entered its Golden Age in 1978 with the release of Space Invaders by Taito, a success that inspired dozens of manufacturers to enter the market.

Colour arcade games became more popular in 1979 and 1980 with the arrival of titles such as Pac-Man. The Golden Age of video arcade games reached its zenith in the 1980s.

The Game Console and Home Computer
With improvements to consoles in the 90s, home video games began to approach the level of graphics seen in arcade games. An increasing number of players would wait for popular arcade games to be adapted for consoles rather than going out. Home computers also became cheaper, more widespread and gained gaming abilities.

Today and Tomorrow
Today's tecnology is changing rapidly. The newest developments include hand-held and mobile phone gaming, huge online games with many players, alternate reality games such as *Second Life*, and games, such as *Farmville* that are linked to social networks.

For more information, the latest games products, and to play a selection of authentic vintage arcade games, visit us at **George's Games** conveniently located at the **Central Entertainment Complex** on Derby Road.
OPENING HOURS: 4-10pm, Sunday-Thursday   12 noon - 12 midnight, Friday and Saturday

PART 4 | **Questions 21-25**

*Read the text and questions below. For each question, mark the letter next to the correct answer **A, B, C** or **D**.*

The Furby Fad

The Furby, a five inch tall doll with bulging eyes and a round mouth, which had a great resemblance to the character from the movie "Gremlins", was a cute enough toy. But how did it become so very popular for a short time, causing a Furby fad?

Part of the interest in the toy was because it displayed lifelike qualities. It was interactive. In particular, it needed nurturing. The toy responded to light, sound and touch and had the ability to learn to speak English. Conversely, it could teach its owner how to speak Furbish, which was a mixture of several language sounds.

However most of its popularity was due to media exposure. The Furby was first demonstrated at the 1998 Toy Fair in New York City. The toy was subsequently mentioned in Time magazine and USA Today and on a number of early morning television shows. The Toy Fair took place in February, but the manufacturer, Tiger Electronics, had planned to release it in October. But because of the media exposure, toy stores began placing large orders for the toy as more and more parents began inquiring about its availability. By the time the toy was released in October, Tiger had already sold out the initial lot of 1.3 million units.

The Furby fad seemed to have been fuelled by the inability of parents to find the toy. When it was not available, everyone needed one. Yet, as soon as they became plentiful, interest in them evaporated.

21. What is the writer doing in this text?

A. trying to show how toys are made

B. presenting the history of a movie character

C. trying to explain the success of a product

D. trying to protect shoppers

22. What did people particularly like about the Furby?

A. It resembled a movie character.

B. It could speak English.

C. It was extremely cute.

D. It seemed alive.

23. The first place anyone saw the Furby was

A. at a toy fair.

B. in a well-known magazine.

C. on morning television.

D. in toy stores.

24. Why does the writer think the Furby became a fad?

A. It was a new idea.

B. It was not widely available on release.

C. It was well advertised.

D. It was affordable.

25. Which best describes the Furby toy?

A. A cute, innovative toy that was extremely popular for a short time.

B. A strange-looking toy that was a huge hit with children despite the doubts of parents.

C. A toy that achieved unexplained and surprising popularity.

D. A modern toy that interacts with children and deserves more popularity than it has.

PART 5 Questions 26-35

Read the text below and choose the correct word for each space. For each question, choose the correct letter **A, B, C** or **D.**

Example answer:

0	A	B	C	D
	▬			

The Work of Jane Goodall

Jane Goodall, the world's leading **(0)** _expert_ on chimpanzees, left England for Africa, **(26)**......................... the age of 23, to visit a friend who had moved **(27)** .... Jane got work as a secretary for Louis Leakey, a Kenyan scientist, **(28)** .... recognised her careful way of working and her interest in animals, and suggested she **(29)** .... him by studying the chimpanzees at Gombe Stream National Park, in Tanzania. She **(30)** .... on to make many important **(31)** .... about chimpanzees which changed two long-standing beliefs of the day: that **(32)** .... humans could construct and use tools, and that chimpanzees were vegetarians. She **(33)** .... the chimpanzees using grass and twigs as tools to remove termites **(34)** .... their mounds, and also hunting and killing smaller monkeys for food. She also observed behaviours that we consider human, **(35)** .... as hugs, kisses, pats on the back, and even tickling.

0.	A. _expert_	B. friend	C. scientist	D. innovator
26.	A. from	B. of	C. on	**D. at**
27.	A. where	**B. there**	C. around	D. out
28.	**A. who**	B. whose	C. when	D. which
29.	A. train	B. use	C. teach	**D. help**
30.	A. started	B. did	C. took	**D. went**
31.	**A. discoveries**	B. laws	C. contacts	D. ideas
32.	A. first	B. mostly	C. usually	**D. only**
33.	A. understood	B. imagined	**C. observed**	D. heard
34.	A. onto	B. outside	C. in	**D. from**
35.	A. which	**B. such**	C. so	D. like

WRITING

PART 1 | Questions 1-5

Here are some sentences about my friend, Keith. For each question, complete the second sentence so that it means the same as the first, **using no more than three words**. Write only the missing words.

> *Example:* *I prefer swimming to cycling.*
> *I like swimming* **more than** *cycling.*

---

1. I asked Keith what he had done on Saturday.

   I asked Keith, "What did .... *you do* .... **on Saturday?"**

2. He told me that he had seen an action film.

   "............ *I saw* .... **an action film", he told me.**

3. Keith prefers action films to dramas.

   Keith likes action films .. *better/more than* .... **he likes dramas.**

4. The film was so good that they couldn't stop talking about it.

   It was .... *such a good* .... **film that they couldn't stop talking about it.**

5. Keith's parents let him stay out until midnight.

   Keith was .... *allowed to stay* .... **out until midnight.**

PAPER 1 - WRITING

PART 2 | Question 6

You just came home from visiting your friend Elizabeth in England. Now, you can't find your MP3 player. Write a card to Elizabeth. In your card, you should

- thank her for hosting you and tell her you had a good time
- ask if you have left your MP3 player at her house
- describe it, and suggest where she should look for it

Write **35-45** words.

PART 3 | Question 7-8

Answer **ONE** of the following questions (**7 or 8**). Write about **100** words. Write the question number at the top of your answer.

Question 7
- This is part of a letter you receive from an English pen friend.

> I'm going to Spain in June! I'm so excited, but I want to lose a bit of weight and get fit in the next few months, so that I feel comfortable at the beach. How can I do it?

- Now write a letter, giving your pen friend some advice.
- Write your **letter** in about 100 words.

Question 8
- Your English teacher has asked you to write a story.
- This is the title for your story:

A Wonderful Surprise

- Write your **story** in about 100 words.

PAPER 2   LISTENING

PART 1   Questions 1-7

There are seven questions in this part. For each question there are three pictures and a short recording. Choose the correct picture and put a tick (✓) in the box below it.

Example: *Where did the woman leave her hat?*

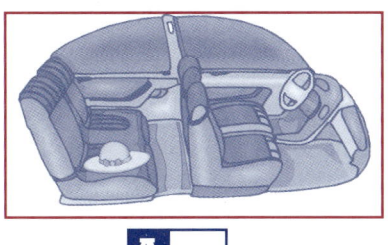      

A ☐   B ✓   C ☐

---

1. What pizza will the man get?

A ✓   B ☐   C ☐

2. Who are they talking about?

A ☐   B ☐   C ✓

3. What is Jan doing now?

A ☐   B ☐   C ✓

4. What is the museum near?

 A

 B ✓

 C

5. What will the weather be like tomorrow night?

 A ✓

 B

 C

6. What kind of transportation is the man talking about?

A

 B ✓

 C

7. For how long was the man on the phone?

ONE HOUR	THIRTY MINUTES	FIFTEEN MINUTES

 A

 B

 C ✓

You will hear part of a radio programme about writers who worked as ambulance drivers in World War One.
For each question, put a tick (✓) in the correct box.

8. How many American authors were ambulance drivers?

A. not less than 23   **A** ✓

B. more than 23   **B**

C. around 4   **C**

9. The connection between ambulance driving and famous writers

A. is present throughout history.   **A**

B. is present in American Universities.   **B**

C. is present during World War I.   **C** ✓

10. What greatly changed the image of the ambulance?

A. that it became too difficult to drive   **A**

B. World War I   **B**

C. the invention of the automobile   **C** ✓

11. Many volunteer ambulance drivers were

A. race-car drivers.   **A**

B. university graduates or students. **B** ✓

C. very wealthy.   **C**

12. What is a reason that made people become ambulance drivers?

A. a desire to avoid danger   **A**

B. a willingness to kill   **B**

C. a wish to participate despite being unfit   **C** ✓

13. Ambulance drivers, but not soldiers

A. were face to face with the war.   **A**

B. had time to think.   **B** ✓

C. were changed by their experiences. **C**

PART 3 **Questions 14-19**

You will hear a radio announcer giving details about an event that is going to take place.
For each question, fill in the missing information in the numbered space.

Fashion Photographs

The name of the visiting photographer: **Mike Jones**

Ages he wants to photograph: **(14)** ...14 to 18.. .

He will feature his photos on his **(15)** ...blog...

He is looking for: a) all shapes, sizes, colours

                          b) all styles of dress

                         c) **(16)** ....girls and boys.................... .

Meeting place: **(17)** ....the square................ in front of the museum.

Meeting time: **(18)** ....10 a.m.............. on Sunday

Inquiry line: **(19)** ....394 944 9025.....................

PART 4 **Questions 20-25**

Look at the six sentences for this part. You will hear a conversation between a boy, William, and a girl, Beth, about after-school sports. Decide if each sentence is correct or incorrect. If it is correct, put a tick (✓) in the box under **A for YES**. If it is not correct, put a tick (✓) in the box under **B for NO**.

	A YES	B NO
20. Beth is good at jumping rope.		✓
21. Beth got a lot of exercise when she went to the sports club.		✓
22. There were only boys playing football.	✓	
23. William thinks Beth would be welcome on the team.	✓	
24. Beth is good at playing football.	✓	
25. William does not think the girls will tease Beth.		✓

Test 10

PART 1 **Questions 1-5**

Look at the text in each question. What does it say? Mark the letter next to the correct explanation **A, B** or **C.**

Example:

0

> ## NO BALL GAMES ALLOWED ON THE GRASS

A. You cannot sit on the grass.

B. Be careful not to damage the grass while playing ball games on it.

C. All ball games are forbidden on the grass.

Example answer: **0** C

1

> Hi Megan,
> Our homework for history class is to read pages 112 - 119.
> I hope you feel better soon!

 B

A. Megan is being punished.

B. Megan probably missed class.

C. Megan is a history teacher.

2

> Tours leave at ten past the hour.
> Please wait here.

 C

This sign

A. announces that the tour has left.

B. gives information about an attraction.

C. marks the place to join a tour.

3

> ## Quiet Please!
> ## Exam in progress
> ### No talking in the hallway!

B

A. You must not speak while taking the exam.

B. Those who are not taking the exam must not talk.

C. The exam is being held in the hallway.

4

> **Phone Message**
> **To:** Robert   **From:** Toby
>
> Hi Robert,
> I am Toby. I called to invite you to my birthday party next Saturday. Call me back for details.

 C

What should Robert do?

A. call Toby if he can go to the party

B. go to the party on Saturday if he is free

C. return the phone call

5

> Dear Charlie,
> Thanks for the wonderful gift! I use the MP3 player every day and like it a lot.

 C

A. Charlie received a gift.

B. The writer recommends an MP3 player.

C. Charlie gave an MP3 player to the writer as a gift.

PAPER 1 - READING

These students (6-10) need to research a topic to write about for their writing class. Below there are some different topics (A-H) that their teacher has suggested. Decide which research topic (**letters A-H**) would most appeal to each student (**numbers 6-10**). Write the correct letter for each number.

6. Mary loves museums, antique shops and car boot sales. She has not travelled much, but wants to in the future. She hopes to be an archeologist one day. Her favourite subjects are art and history.

6	G

7. Andre is a bookworm. He knows a bit about almost everything. If he was on a trivia game show, he would probably win. He is often bored in class, however, and wishes he could learn something about a subject he's never heard of before or a new invention or discovery.

7	B

8. Anna loves fashion, clothes, hairstyles and make-up. Sometimes she spends more time getting ready for school in the morning than she spends doing her homework. She wants to be famous.

8	F

9. Miguel's parents keep getting jobs in different countries. He has already lived in 5 counties and speaks 3 different languages. He likes meeting people but is tired of having to make new friends every few years. Sometimes he feels that this isn't fair.

9	H

10. Harry likes all sorts of aircraft. He wants to be a pilot, or perhaps an astronaut. He enjoys his history and maths lessons, but doesn't like science at all.

10	A

SUGGESTED TOPICS

A. The Wright Brothers
Read about the lives of these pioneers of aviation. How did their background influence their amazing achievements? How were they influenced by their time? How exactly did they achieve the first powered human flight?

B. New Animal Discoveries
You might think today we know all there is to know about the world around us - but do we really? Find out about the newest animals discovered by science. What strange creatures have been found last year in the deepest ocean, remote jungles, or under the polar ice?

C. Man's Best Friend
Domestic dogs come in all shapes and sizes today, but most likely, they all developed from the wolf! Trace the history of the domestic dog, and explain why this great friendship began, and how we've ended up with so many different shapes and sizes of dogs.

D. The Most Popular Sport
What is the most popular sport in the world? What do you think? Find some data that supports your idea, and then find out about the sport, some significant names that have taken part in the sport, and the reasons for its popularity.

E. The Solar System
Find out what makes our solar system tick. You will draw on your knowledge of Physics to explain why the planets rotate the sun, why moons exist, why Saturn has rings, and even why there is day and night.

F. Holly Golightly
This role, in *Breakfast at Tiffany's*, launched Audrey Hepburn's career. Hepburn as Holly, carrying an oversized cigarette holder, is considered one of the most iconic images of 20th century American cinema. One of the dresses she wore in the film sold at auction on the 5th December, 2006 for £467,200. Find out about the character, and the actress.

G. Prehistoric London
Find out what was there before today's capital city that we all know. You will find information about the digs that took place before various modern buildings and the underground were built.

H. Migration
People all over the world are moving, more than at any other time in history. Why is that? What are the implications? You can explore this issue from the perspective of the individual, a society or the world as a whole.

PART 3   Questions 11-20

Look at the statements below about exams. Read the text below to decide if each statement is correct or incorrect. If it is correct, mark **A**. If it is incorrect, mark **B**.

11. It is not normal to feel stressed about exams.   **11** **B**

12. Stress can come from a fear of failure.   **12** **A**

13. Becoming very stressed can be bad for you.   **13** **A**

14. Everyone reacts to stress in the same way.   **14** **B**

15. Some people do well under stress.   **15** **A**

16. Stress is never helpful.   **16** **B**

17. If you know what to expect, you will feel less worried.   **17** **A**

18. It doesn't matter when you study.   **18** **B**

19. If you breathe more quickly, you will calm down.   **19** **B**

20. A healthy diet will not help you to handle stress.   **20** **B**

Can I avoid getting stressed before an exam?

Taking exams is bound to be stressful because of what is at stake. You may be feeling a weight of expectation from your family, school, university or workplace to succeed. You may be afraid you are not good enough, or have not worked hard enough. You may be scared of letting yourself down, or that you'll miss out on a job, university place or career move.

If your stress levels rise too high for too long, it can be harmful both to you and to your chances. Everybody's stress 'threshold' is different. A situation that is too much for one person to tolerate may be stimulating to another. Controlled at the right level, however, stress can work to your advantage, because it can help you to produce your peak performance.

Here's what you can do to keep exam stress at a healthy level:

Be organised
If you know exactly what you are facing, this will go a long way towards putting your mind at ease. Get hold of the right information from the start. Make sure you know how you will be examined and what you'll be examined on. Catch up with anything you have missed right away.

Make a Timetable
Take time to plan a revision timetable that is realistic and still flexible, and linked to your exam timetable, so you revise subjects in the right order. In planning it, give yourself clear priorities and try to balance your revision with other demands on your time - meals, sleep, chores or other commitments, as well as time for relaxing. Identify your best time of day for studying.

Learn to Relax
Stress can make you start breathing with quick, shallow breaths and make your heart beat faster than usual. If this happens, try to be aware of how quickly you are breathing. If it's one breath every couple of seconds, take a deep breath and start counting steadily. Breathe out slowly and try to get the last of the breath out in about five seconds. Carry on doing this until you are doing it naturally.

Keep Healthy
Exercise is an excellent way of coping with stress. Try to get 20 minutes per day. Sleep is critical - if you lack sleep, even small things will be stressful. Of course, you must eat right too! Don't stop taking care of yourself.

Read the text and questions below. For each question, mark the letter next to the correct answer **A, B, C or D.**

The Origin of Jeans

In 1853, the California gold rush was in full swing and everyday items were in short supply. Levi Strauss, a 24-year-old German immigrant, left New York for San Francisco with a small supply of dry goods with the intention of opening a branch of his brother's New York dry goods business. Shortly after his arrival, a prospector wanted to know what Mr. Strauss was selling. When Strauss told him he had rough canvas cloth to use for tents and wagon covers, the prospector said, "You should have brought trousers!", because he couldn't find a pair of trousers strong enough to last.

Levi Strauss had the canvas made into work trousers. Miners liked the trousers, but complained that the fabric was not very comfortable and tended to chafe. Levi Strauss substituted the canvas with a twilled cotton cloth from France called "serge de Nimes." The fabric later became known as denim and the trousers were nicknamed blue jeans. Then Levi Strauss and Nevada tailor David Jacobs co-patented the process of putting small metal rivets in places such as the sides of the pockets that needed extra strength. On May 20, 1873, they received U.S.Patent No.139,121. This date is now considered the official birthday of "blue jeans."

But why were they called blue jeans? Denim is unique in its singular connection with one colour. It is made from thread that is traditionally dyed with the blue pigment obtained from indigo dye. Indigo was linked with practical fabrics and work clothing. The durability of indigo as a colour and its darkness of tone made it a good choice when frequent washing was not possible.

---

21. What is the purpose of this text?

    A. to sell a product

    B. to solve a problem

    C. to argue a point

    D. to inform

22. What was Levi Strauss' job?

    A. He was a clothes designer.

    B. He was a prospector.

    C. He was selling textiles and clothing.

    D. He was selling tools for gold mining.

23. What problem did the prospectors have?

    A. There were no trousers in California.

    B. They did not like Levi's product.

    C. Their clothes were not stylish.

    D. Their clothes wore out quickly.

24. Where did the word 'denim' come from?

    A. the name of a French fabric

    B. the indigo colour

    C. David Jacobs, the tailor, thought of it

    D. Levi Strauss invented it

25. Which best describes indigo dye?

    A. A long lasting, practical colour that did not show dirt

    B. A colour used on all kinds of fabric to make the fabric stronger.

    C. A very rare and desirable colour that was difficult to create.

    D. An affordable dark colour that was only used by poor people.

PART 5 **Questions 26-35**

Read the text below and choose the correct word for each space. For each question, choose the correct letter **A, B, C or D.**

Example answer:

0	A	B	C	D

The Cheetah

The cheetah is an unusual member **(0) of** the cat family that has many **(26)** .... characteristics. It is ideally suited to its African grassland habitat, but faces challenges to its survival in the **(27)** ....

It is exceptional in its speed, while lacking strong climbing abilities. It is the fastest land animal, reaching speeds **(28)** .... 112 and 120 kilometres per hour, in short bursts. It **(29)** .... the ability to accelerate from 0 to 100 kilometres per hour in three seconds, faster than most supercars. **(30)** .... the cheetah is a sprinter it cannot keep **(31)** .... its amazing speeds for long periods of time.

The cheetah is a vulnerable species. Of all the big cats, it is the **(32)** .... able to adapt to new environments. Indeed, all cheetahs are so closely related that they have very similar genes, **(33)** .... makes them susceptible to diseases. They have always proved difficult to breed in captivity, although recently a few zoos have managed to **(34)** .... in this. Once widely hunted for its fur, the cheetah now suffers more from the loss of **(35)** .... habitat and prey.

0.	A. *of*	B. from	C. in	D. among
26.	A. scarce	B. unique	C. typical	D. dangerous
27.	A. past	B. future	C. today	D. now
28.	A. between	B. of	C. through	D. below
29.	A. is	B. makes	C. does	D. has
30.	A. Despite	B. Nevertheless	C. Although	D. Even
31.	A. with	B. up	C. on	D. for
32.	A. least	B. less	C. only	D. little
33.	A. it	B. what	C. which	D. and
34.	A. overcome	B. win	C. achieve	D. succeed
35.	A. the	B. neither	C. both	D. either

WRITING

PART 1 **Questions 1-5**

Here are some sentences about me and my family. For each question, complete the second sentence so that it means the same as the first, <u>using no more than three words</u>. Write only the missing words.

Example: *I prefer swimming to cycling.*
I like swimming <u>more than</u> cycling.

---

1. My brother started playing the violin 5 years ago.

   My brother .....*has been playing*......... **the violin for 5 years.**

2. My father is a musician. He is the best guitar player I have ever seen!

   My father ....*is better than*......... **all the other guitar players I have seen so far!**

3. My brother told me he wanted a scarf for his birthday.

   " .....*I want / I would like*..... **a scarf for my birthday" said my brother.**

4. I very rarely go into the city centre, so I don't know where to shop.

   I am ....*not used to*......... **shopping in the city centre.**

5. My mother told me the high street would be more affordable than the mall.

   My mother told me the mall would ......*be less*......... **affordable than the high street.**

PART 2 | Question 6

You recently bought a T-shirt from a company on the internet. You are not at all happy with the purchase.
Write an e-mail to the company to complain. Include the following points:

- took too long to arrive
- fits well, but is not good quality
- would like a refund

Write **35-45** words.

PART 3 | Question 7-8

Answer **ONE** of the following questions (**7 or 8**). Write about **100** words. Write the question number at the top of your answer.

Question 7
- This is part of a letter you received from an English pen friend.

> I'm so excited to be coming to visit you this summer!
> What do I need to bring with me?

- Now write a letter, telling your pen friend what he or she needs to bring.
- Write your **letter** in about 100 words.

Question 8
- Your English teacher has asked you to write a story.
- This is the title for your story:

A Frightening Experience

- Write your **story** in about 100 words.

PAPER 2   LISTENING

PART 1   Questions 1-7

There are seven questions in this part. For each question there are three pictures and a short recording. Choose the correct picture and put a tick (✓) in the box below it.

Example: *Where did the woman leave her hat?*

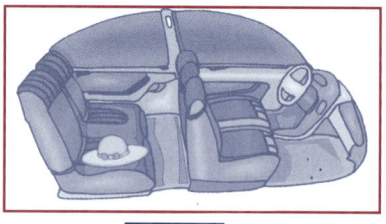

A

B ✓

C

---

1. Which jumper does the man like?

A

B

C ✓

2. What is the current weather?

A ✓

B

C

3. At which time is the plumber available?

3 o'clock	12 o'clock	5.30 o'clock
A ✓	**B**	**C**

4. Where was the book?

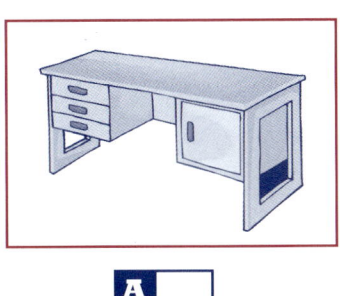

A

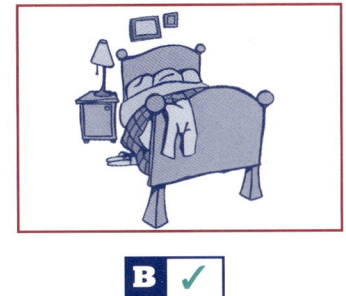

B ✓

C

5. What's the woman wearing?

A

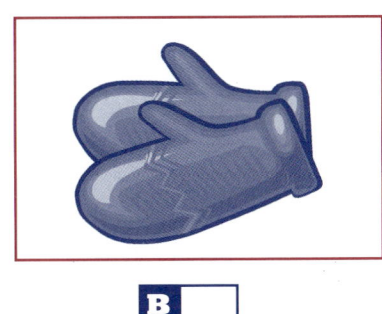

B

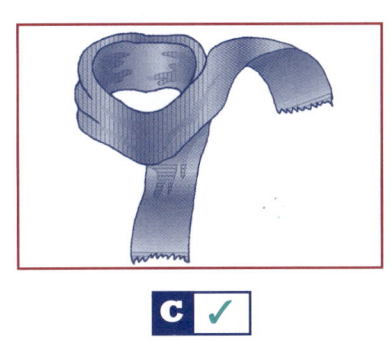

C ✓

6. Which is the woman's handbag?

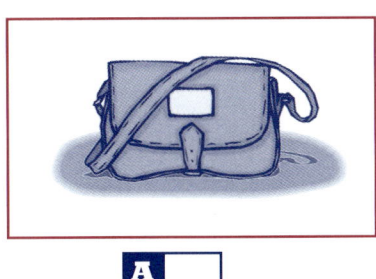

A

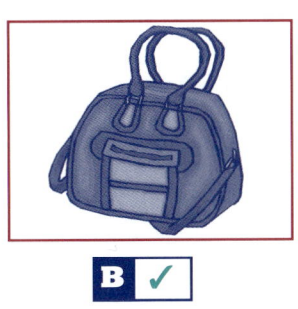

B ✓

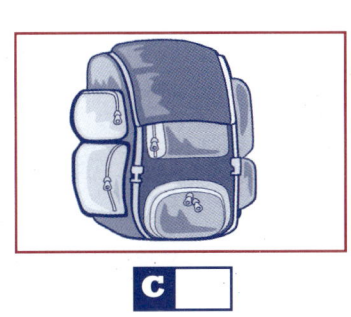

C

7. Where are they going?

A ✓

B

C

PART 2   Questions 8-13

You will hear a radio interview with Mr. Davies about the game of conkers. For each question, put a tick (✓) in the correct box.

8. Conkers is

A. a playground game.

B. a seed from a tree.

C. a holiday in the autumn.

A	✓
B	
C	

9. Mr. Davies is sad because

A. the game can only be played in the autumn.

B. fewer children now play the game.

C. the game has been completely forgotten.

A	
B	✓
C	

10. A conker is

A. the winner of the game.

B. a children's game.

C. a seed from a tree.

A	
B	
C	✓

11. The children

A. purchase their conkers.

B. find conkers if they are lucky.

C. make their own conkers.

A	
B	
C	✓

12. Someone loses the game when

A. his or her conker is hit.

B. his or her conker is destroyed.

C. he or she has more than 10 points.

A	
B	✓
C	

13. A winning conker

A. takes the score of its victim.

B. is replaced by another conker.

C. is not used again.

A	✓
B	
C	

PART 3 — Questions 14-19

You will hear a radio announcer giving details about a contest that is being held. For each question, fill in the missing information in the numbered space.

Photography Contest

Contest is being held by: North Counties **(14)** ....rescue..

You should submit photos of: **(15)** ....your pet.................................... .

Send submissions by email, to the address: **(16)** ..northcountiesrescue@gmail.com.......

Photos must be sent by the: **(17)** ......12th September (4pm).................

Winners will receive a £25 **(18)** ....gift certificate...................

Also, the winning photos will be used in a **(19)** ....calendar...............................

PART 4 — Questions 20-25

Look at the six sentences for this part. You will hear a conversation between a boy, Harry, and his Mum, about the marks he got on a test. Decide if each sentence is correct or incorrect. If it is correct, put a tick (✓) in the box under **A for YES**. If it is not correct, put a tick (✓) in the box under **B for NO**.

	A YES	B NO
20. Harry had an exciting day.		✓
21. Harry wants to talk to his mum about his day.		✓
22. Harry's mum looks in his bag even though he doesn't want her to.		✓
23. Harry's mum is very angry about the exam result.		✓
24. Harry's mum thinks he studied hard enough.	✓	
25. Harry doesn't mind if his mum calls his teacher		✓